The Office Book™
DESIGN SERIES

Open Office Space

John Pile
Consulting Editor: Edith Siroto

Facts On File

Facts On File, Inc.
460 Park Avenue South
New York, New York 10016

A QUARTO BOOK

First published in 1984 by Facts On File, Inc.
460 Park Avenue South, New York, N.Y. 10016

Library of Congress Cataloging in Publication Data
Pile, John F.
Open office space.
(The Office book design series)
Bibliography: p. 93
Includes index.
1. Office layout. I. Title. II. Series.
HF5547.P54   1983   747'.8523   83-5654

ISBN 0-87196-782-0
ISBN 0-87196-783-9 (pbk.)

OPEN OFFICE SPACE
was produced and prepared by
Quarto Marketing Ltd.
212 Fifth Avenue, New York, NY 10010

Editor: Marta Hallett
Art Director: Richard Boddy
Managing Editor: Naomi Black
Editorial Assistant: Mary Forsell

Typeset by BPE Graphics, Inc.
Color separations by Hong Kong Scanner Craft Company Ltd.
Printed and bound in Hong Kong by Leefung-Asco Printers Ltd.

C O N T E N T S

Introduction

From the time the idea first surfaced, open planning (or its European parallel, office landscape) has been a matter for lively discussion. People tend to take sides, for or against, seeing this as a route to a better world of offices, or as a foolish fad according to their own background and prejudices. A substantial literature of journal articles and books has accumulated explaining, supporting, and attacking the open plan concept.

Most of this literature has been aimed at the professional audience of architects, interior designers, and office planners who are directly responsible for the way offices are laid out and built. Naturally this literature has been somewhat technical in its point of view and has appeared in the magazines that reach the appropriate professions and in books that assume the reader is actively involved in office planning.

Office workers generally know about open planning through direct exposure. A visit to an open office, a job in an organization that has adopted open planning, or rumors about an upcoming move to a new location where "there will be no private offices" generate visceral reactions lacking in any reference to the ideas that lie behind this concept.

While professionals plan offices and advise their clients on what planning approach to use, final decisions are generally in the hands of managers, executives, the people that designers call "the client." The client can express preferences, listen to professional advice, and approve or disapprove, but can only do so intelligently on the basis of some knowledge about the alternatives available. Open planning is a concept with a theoretical base, it is now in use with many versions that share openness but differ in other ways.

This book is not a "how-to" manual for professionals nor a "do-it-yourself" for amateurs. Rather, it is intended as a briefing on what open planning is about, where and how it began, and how it is now practiced. It does not suggest that this is the only form of planning, perfect for every situation, but it aims to provide a basis of understanding that will support reasonable decisions about when open planning should be used, and what form of open plan should be selected to serve a particular situation. Executives and managers who must decide about a new office, those who are to manage and direct the use of open plan space, and the staff that will work in open office space should find a basis of understanding here that will make the open office seem like something more than a trendy fad.

All the evidence suggests that the use of open planning is on the increase, for reasons which are discussed in detail further on. A resistance to open planning, often called a "backlash" has developed, largely in response to badly conceived and poorly managed open projects. Backlash or no, there will be more and more open offices; therefore, it is very much in the interest of users and managers alike to have an understanding of open planning that will be a defense against poor planning and that will aid and support the planners work in arriving at a maximally successful project.

Office work and office equipment are in a period of rapid change. The systems and the projects shown here represent a cross section of the *current* scene. Still, beyond the details of currently available equipment, this book addresses the general points concerning all office design and about open office design in particular. The best projects of ten, or even twenty, years ago stand up well in comparison with work being done now. The best recent work illustrated here will set the pace for quite a few years ahead.

There can be no substitute for visiting, or better yet for actually working in, open office space of top quality to develop an understanding of what this approach can do. Decision makers should actually experience the workings of an open office as an extension and supplement to what can be discovered from the pages of this book.

John Pile

History

Offices throughout history have generally been rooms of moderate size. The prototype was the library or study used by an aristocratic "gentleman" or the consulting room of professionals. Such an office is, by nature, private. A secretary or assistant would occupy another, possibly smaller space, but this also would be private. With the advent of larger organizations, businesses, governmental agencies, banks, and brokerages, another kind of office appeared—an office for staff with several people sharing one space. Older office buildings are designed to provide both of these kinds of offices—individual private offices for managers and executives, and rooms shared by several coworkers for staff, clerks, typists, and bookkeepers.

The shared office in larger organizations then grew into a large "general office" or "bullpen" where dozens, even hundreds, of workers could be seated at desks in neat and often seemingly endless rows. Executives and middle managers could be placed in private or semiprivate rooms at the perimeter. This sort of office is sometimes called "American" because it became commonplace in the United States for insurance companies, mail-order houses, and governmental agencies that employed a hive of clerical workers. In Europe, the pattern of many smaller rooms arranged along corridors remained the norm until recently.

The open bullpen is not what the modern term "open office planning" refers to, and it is not what this book is concerned with. The modern open office is the result of a particular planning approach that was first tried around 1960. It was introduced in Germany with the catchy name "office landscape" on the basis of theoretical studies by the brothers Eberhard and Wolfgang Schnelle. These men were leaders of

Drawing courtesy John Pile

The open office of the turn of the century, with "work stations" in golden oak. The manager's desk, foreground, is larger and placed in sight of all the "general office" desks. Also note the filing and storage systems on the desks and in the cabinets against the back and side walls.

the management consultant firm Quickborner Team, named for the town of Quickborn, a suburb of Hamburg where it was based.

Quickborner studies found that office work was inhibited and confused by the illogical layout of offices: People who needed constant communication often were located far from one another, and people with no need for contact sometimes were squeezed into one small room. Status expression and formal organizational charts determined office plans, while practical and logical needs were ignored. As a solution, the Quickborner Team proposed and then demonstrated a type of office that was a large space totally free of walls, partitions, and corridors. In this "open landscape" office personnel could be placed as the flow of communication might require. Paper flow, and visual and spoken contact were made easy, managers were made accessible, working groups could feel a sense of cohesiveness, and changes and replanning were facilitated.

Privacy in the office landscape was not totally ignored but became a matter of movable screens placed to block sight-lines as desired. For management, the extra area made distances to other work places longer. Special care was devoted to acoustical matters dealing with problems of noise and the more subtle problems of "speech privacy," that is, matters of overhead conversation.

Office landscape plans are not geometric; rather, they are a somewhat free, seemingly random scramble. But this free pattern is very carefully planned on the basis of methodical studies of communication, which lead to charts of "interaction" patterns. There are lounge areas for use by all personnel, and segregated storage areas, removed from the work space. These planning practices are set out as a series of "rules" for planning, including the most controversial rule, that there must be *no* private, partitioned offices, even for top executives. This last rule prevents the development of a two-class situation.

Landscape planning came into extensive use in Germany first and then in other European countries (particularly in the Scandinavian countries and in England), and has been used in many projects in the United States as well. The strict application of the rules of landscape planning has, in recent years, given way to a less doctrinaire approach that has been encouraged by the development of new types of office furniture generally referred to as "systems furniture." The term "open planning" as it is used here is to be understood as referring to this freer approach; although "landscaped" offices are also to be viewed as a particular kind of open plan.

In the United States, the Quickborner approach was received with some skepticism. A number of experimental installations yielded inconclusive results as to success—enthusiasts reported dramatic successes while doubters told horror stories about noise and confusion and the disgruntled state of executives deprived of their traditional names on doors, corner windows, and Bigelows. An American inventor-researcher named Robert Propst is usually credited with the development of a new sort of office furniture that has been a key to making open planning popular in the U.S. Propst had been developing office furniture of an unconventional sort for use in conventional offices before the ideas of landscape planning surfaced. Propst's "Action Office" did away with desks and credenzas and substituted work surfaces, storage units, and other components to be hung on walls (together with freestanding tables and work units).

When open landscape concepts came to the U.S., Propst

added screen panels to take the place of walls so that work and storage units of an "Action Office" would have a place to hang. The resulting system makes possible a range of levels of privacy and compartmentation, provides for varied equipment in compact spaces, and permits rearrangement with a minumum of trouble and wasted time. This kind of furniture system was quickly imitated by other manufacturers while designers developed other systems, quite different in character, until there are now literally hundreds of office systems to serve open plan needs.

Debates over the merits of open planning, discussions of whether this is here to stay or merely a fad seem to have died away. Open planning *is* here to stay, but there is also a general recognition that it is not the only, the universal, and inevitable solution to all office problems. The use of conventional planning (that is, partitioned, individual rooms) survives and has been, in some ways, enlivened by ideas generated from open planning. Also, contrary to the theoretical views of landscape originators, combinations of open and conventional planning have gained increasing acceptance. Some product systems even provide for a degree of interchangeability or at least compatibility between open and partitioned approaches so that varied and changing needs can be dealt with as time passes.

Office planning has not "settled down" into accepted patterns, because ongoing events are constantly challenging anything that might seem like established norms. The most striking pressures come from the group of related developments that are discussed under such topic heads as "Office of the Future"—the impact of computer-related techniques that have moved into every aspect of office work more rapidly, more effectively, and more pervasively than even the most sanguine futurists were predicting just a few years ago. The results of this revolution are not yet sorted out—new equipment is made obsolete by newer equipment almost daily, changing the nature of office work in ways that are almost impossible to follow as a result. The physical environment of the office, however rapidly updated, always seems to lag behind. Office workers at every level from top executive to basic support staff note that present norms quickly give way to still newer patterns.

Open planning is particularly suited to this era of rapid change because of its inherent flexibility. Varying levels of privacy, furniture changes to accommodate new equipment, techniques for easy rearrangement of wiring and lighting, are all part of the current practice of open planning. Even the question of whether openness is really desirable can be dealt with, since open systems provide for, paradoxically, enclosure when and where it is needed.

With a growing proportion of the total workforce now involved in office work (it now accounts for more than 50 percent of total working hours), questions about "productivity" in office work are receiving increasing attention. Measurements used for factory and agricultural work do not apply well to measurement of office productivity. Recent research is moving toward measurements that have, at least, some superiority over pure guesswork in this area. As a result, new approaches to office planning and design are now subject to more objective evaluation than was possible in the past. Indications are that open planning, in one form or another, will prove to be basic in the development of office scenes that truly serve their users well.

Open Planning in Current Practice

While debates continue about the merits of open office planning, acceptance has become widespread. Many office furniture systems are designed to be useful in open offices, while some are appropriate *only* in open situations. Office planners and designers, well aware of some of the open plan advantages, propose open planning to their clients and explain its merits so persuasively that even doubters are often converted to enthusiasts. Still, for each office project, it is pertinent to ask whether open planning is *really* suitable, or possibly appropriate, to only portions of an office.

Before reviewing the case in favor of open planning, I should admit that there are situations where a conventional, fully partitioned layout is still preferable. In general, this applies wherever maximum privacy—visual and acoustic—is of major importance to each office inhabitant. An obvious example is a suite of medical offices or the office of a psychiatrist. Law offices are generally fully partitioned so that each partner can meet with clients in a setting that suggests total confidentiality. At the same time, some parts of law offices—work areas for clerks and secretaries, possibly junior partners' offices as well— probably could be open even though tradition may dictate otherwise.

Managers and executives often express a desire for confidential privacy, but this demand needs to be measured against the advantages of open plan. Confidential privacy can always be provided for in conference and meeting rooms, accommodating occasional needs for closed-door isolation for a number of users. Full enclosure for each person with intermittent needs for full privacy is usually a waste of space and money. Also, many enclosed offices are not fully private since voices can be heard clearly through walls of common

A typical open office with well-planned lighting, communications, and acoustic treatments. The plants sprinkled throughout the room are very much a part of the "office landscape" tradition. (Montgomery Ward headquarters, Chicago, Illinois)

Photograph by Hedrich Blessing, courtesy Sidney Rodgers Associates

drywall construction and the panels of many partition systems. In fact, demands for privacy are often disguised desires for what is believed to be the elevated status conferred by a totally enclosed room.

In contrast, certain types of work that require quiet and concentration may justify provision of enclosed space quite aside from status level. Creative writers or scientific researchers may have reasonable claims for this kind of privacy, but here again it is important to review how much real need there is. Shared access to a few closed cubicles to serve occasional needs combined with open work places for daily use to allow for easy communication is often a better solution.

There can also be more intangible reasons for ruling out open planning. The most common case of this kind is an organization whose head is deeply opposed to the ideas of an open plan for whatever reason: honest doubts, simple conservatism, or fears of lost status. And if the chief dislikes the idea, his or her attitude tends to spread through an organization and to generate all sorts of spurious objections that defeat the concept before it is put into use or undermine its success when tried.

An often-suggested compromise that has come into fairly common use is open planning for parts of a space and partitioned offices for other parts, each planning system used, presumably, where it is most appropriate. While it may seem logical, this kind of mixed planning has serious problems. As mentioned earlier, the traditional practice of providing private offices for managers and bullpens for staff tends to create a two-class society of "officers" and "enlisted men," separate and somewhat hostile to each other. If open planning is used for the equivalent of the bullpen, it can improve that part of an office, although nothing will have changed the two-class organizational structure. If closed offices are provided regardless of status level, on the basis of need alone, planning difficulties are likely to arise (enclosed boxes scattered about in odd places), and those in the enclosed spaces many acquire an unintended elevation of status. For these reasons, open planning generally proves to be most successful when it is accepted for *all* work stations within a given facility. Open planning for a whole department, a whole floor, or a whole building, even when conventional planning is used elsewhere by the firm or organization, may sometimes be reasonable, but care must be taken to avoid the sense that the open plan facility is in some way inferior. When the top executive offices are open, no problems will arise, but a conventional executive area generates desires for enclosure that work against the success of open planning used elsewhere.

Having noted the reservations about the use of open

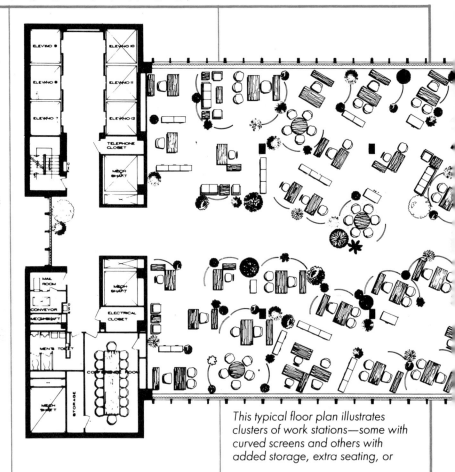

This typical floor plan illustrates clusters of work stations—some with curved screens and others with added storage, extra seating, or

planning (by itself or in combination with conventional planning), it is now necessary to face the question of why open plan offices are used at all. The originators of office landscape defined a very specific list of benefits. As their methods have come to be modified, some of these benefits are not fully realized while other, unplanned-for merits have surfaced. Open planning at its best can offer all of the benefits listed below. In practice, most installations achieve a few of these virtues fully, others to some more limited degree.

- Office workers in an open plan space achieve better communication than in partitioned offices. People can talk to one another, use visual signals, and pass papers from hand to hand without going in and out of separate spaces and through corridors.

- Groups working together develop a "team" sense through seeing each other in a physical grouping and come to understand each other's work. They can "cover" for an absent person and generally cooperate more naturally than when isolated in separate spaces.

- Managers are not made a separate class through isolation

Plan courtesy Sidney Rodgers Associates

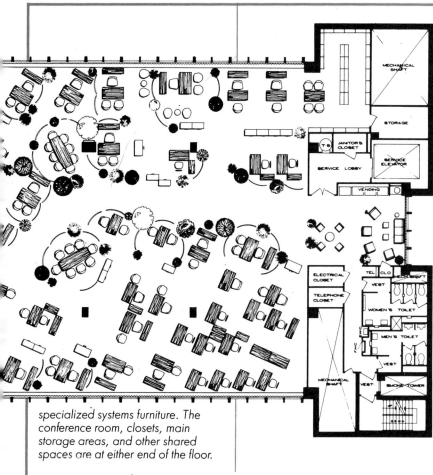

specialized systems furniture. The conference room, closets, main storage areas, and other shared spaces are at either end of the floor.

and so can direct and supervise their staff naturally; they will be seen as mentors rather than as task masters.

- Changes in the arrangement of work stations to accommodate alterations in work patterns are relatively easy to make (no partitions to tear down and rebuild). Changes in furniture and equipment within work stations are easy to make, to adjust to individual needs.

- Large open spaces are easier and less expensive to light, heat, and cool than many, separate, private rooms.

- Electrical, telephone, and other communications wiring can be provided for and changed more easily.

- With proper acoustical treatment (ceiling, carpeted floors, and background sound systems), the activity noises in an open office provide a better acoustical environment than the silence of a closed office combined with overheard conversations leaking through partitions, above ceilings, and through ducts.

- There is a major cost saving in the original construction by eliminating walls and doors. This may be partly or totally

offset by the extra cost of furniture system work stations, but saving is possible if that is made a significant goal.

- There is a major cost saving each time a layout rearrangement is undertaken. A major change can often take place overnight without construction costs and lost working time. With each layout change, savings accumulate, so over the life of a facility, savings from this source and from original construction are certain to make open planning economically desirable.

- There *may* be a saving in floor space requirements leading to a saving in rent or construction cost. Open planning can always make such a saving possible if desired, but many projects use this advantage to provide improved amenity and a "cushion" of space for future expansion.

- Given good planning and equipment, users *like* open offices better than warrens of closed cubicles. This leads to improved morale, to a reduction in absenteeism and worker turnover, and to improvement in total office "productivity."

With such a list of potential advantages, it is reasonable to ask why anyone might still have doubts about the validity of this approach. There is, as mentioned in the Introduction, "backlash" opposition to the use of open planning. It seems to arise from situations where open plan projects have been badly designed or unwisely imposed in inappropriate situations. Backlash centers around objections based on bad experiences, some of which are discussed below.

- A loss of privacy has made some aspect of work impossible. This usually describes a situation in which open planning should never have been considered in the first place. It might describe a situation in which some private cubicles or conference rooms should have been provided, but were not.

- Noise and overheard conversations from adjacent work places are a major source of annoyance. This usually indicates that proper acoustic provisions were not planned or were dropped in a misguided effort at economy. All open plan projects require special acoustic measures, usually including a background sound system. Such systems are often unwisely omitted. They are even opposed in the belief that they are in some way objectionable.

- An open work station is totally inferior to a private office. This complaint usually comes from someone who regards a private office, perhaps a newly won "perk" or one hoped for in the near future, as a status marker of great significance. Deprivation is then converted into irrational complaints.

This work station uses elements from the Storwall System, George Nelson design. Although the slatted partitions allow for more light, they still offer a modicum of visual privacy.

- The open office is a vast wasteland or hive of tiny stalls, dehumanizing and depressing. This is a fairly accurate description of some poorly designed projects, or those designed without much thought for the impact of an impersonal "landscape" on the individual worker. Similar criticism will apply to conventional offices planned with parallel impersonality. Open planning, at its best, makes excellent provisions for "personalization" of the individual workplace and provides for division of work space into units that are comfortable and comprehensible to the individual user.

A number of the advantages of open planning—economy, flexibility, and improvements in productivity—do not impinge on the individual office worker and are significant only to management in a rather abstract way. It is important to the success of a project that some of the other potential advantages, improved amenity (with more space) and easy communication for example, be realized so individual workers can easily recognize a positive component of the system.

Open plan projects in current use may be divided into several categories that can be arranged in a sequence according to their relationship to the theoretical position of the office landscape originators. At one end of the scale are projects planned in the ways developed by the Quickborner Team— often projects in which that organization is involved. At the opposite extreme are projects totally without theoretical objectives, simply planned without partitioning and therefore, unquestionably "open." The theoretical basics of open planning require the application of a methodology that is not necessarily made visible in finished results but underlies the effectiveness of the approach. The theory behind the methodology assumes that any office is simply a forum for communication— communication that should lead to valid managerial decision making and should facilitate the processing of the routine tasks that the office exists to perform. A study of communication must therefore precede any meaningful planning.

A communication study begins with a form issued to each office worker (from top executive to junior clerk) calling for an accurate report of all communications, in- and outbound, by word of mouth, phone, or paper, with any other person in the organization. A time period of about two weeks is usually considered adequate for this study. The statistical resultant is then processed into a matrix chart, similar to the mileage or fare charts of maps and timetables, which gives a numerical value to the level of communication between each possible pairing of individuals within the organization. The raw count of number of communications may be converted to levels such as "never," "seldom," "occasional," "frequent," "very frequent," and "constant" with each given a numerical value. The study may be simplified by grouping individuals into "work groups" or "departments" to reduce the number of individual units entered in the matrix chart. However organized, the matrix is intended to display figures indicating the *need* for proximity as evidenced by level of communication.

The point here is to avoid placement of work stations solely on the basis of organizational chart relationships and to substitute reality of function. Thus, rather than placing all sales personnel together, all accountants together, and all vice presidents together simply because of titles, available data indicate which persons or groups should be close for genuine, functional reasons. Vice presidents may need to be close, but they may also need to be near certain sales or accounting personnel. A project team may include people from many job classifications and departments who should be grouped rather than scattered. The numerical data on the matrix chart is converted to other charts that show clusters of people grouped on the basis of communication needs. Links between clusters are charted, and clusters are diagrammed in terms of floor space requirements. This leads to other charts, often called "bubble diagrams," in which floor area is displayed as an abstract, flexible commodity that can then be adjusted into patterns that relate to actual available floor space.

Work stations are then laid out and questions of privacy needs considered in terms of actual sight-lines and acoustic distances. When this planning approach is rigorously applied, patterns of furniture arrangement are likely to be irregular, nongeometric, and as seen in plan, seemingly random. In fact, the patterns are closely tailored to real needs rather than to an imposed order or aesthetic. Intended users of the space are invited to participate in the planning process criticizing proposed plans, altering and adjusting them in cooperation with the planner until a scheme satisfactory to all is developed. This latter technique both refines the plan to match the direct experience of users and, at the same time, tends to secure support and approval through participation.

Such landscape planning also usually strives for a minimum of screening and enclosure, for a minimum of storage at the workplace (preferring central files and supply rooms), and for open rest and coffee-break areas conveniently available to all workers. It is also part of the landscape tradition to provide live plants as visual screens, area dividers, circulation directors, and as a visual amenity. Plants are very much a part of the "office landscape" but are not the primary reason for its name which refers rather to the natural placement of things on the basis of real-life processes—as with the trees, rocks, and streams in a natural landscape.

This kind of landscape planning has been subject to a number of modifications over the years and most open plan projects are, in practice, variants of this basic concept. In the United States in particular, landscape projects seem to offer too little storage space at the workplace and too little visual privacy. Furniture designers and manufacturers have hastened to deal with both problems, motivated perhaps, by self-interest in that their solutions involve the use of the complex office furniture usually called "systems furniture." Systems usually provide some visual privacy with screens or panels, which may

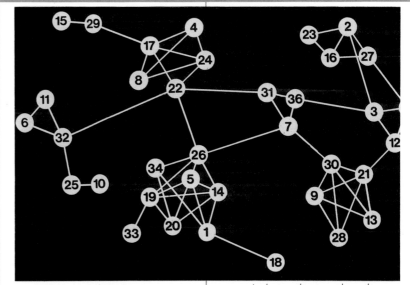

A cluster chart, such as the one above, illustrates the functional relationships of many work stations, based on their communication needs. Links between the clusters are diagrammed in terms of volume of interaction.

An orderly open plan area at Weyerhauser headquarters in Tacoma, Washington, uses the Knoll Zapf system. The floor-to-ceiling windows fulfill both aesthetic and lighting needs.

Plan courtesy Herman Miller, Inc.   Photograph © Jaime Ardiles-Arce, courtesy Knoll International, Inc.

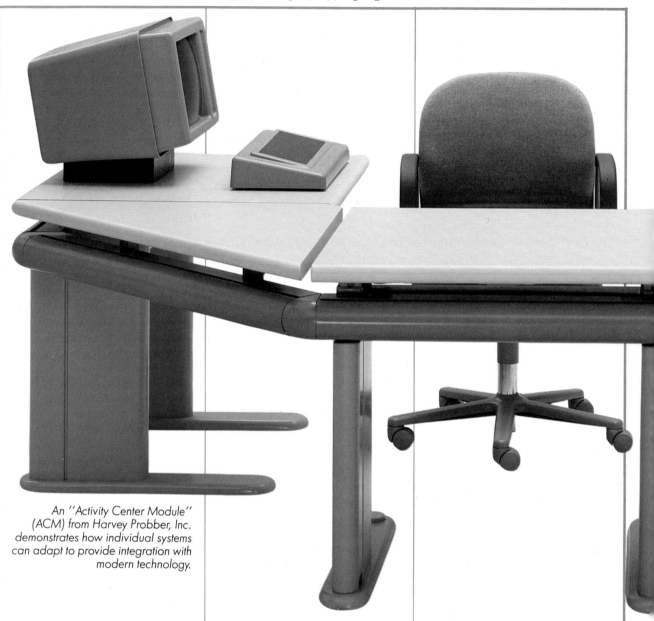

An "Activity Center Module" (ACM) from Harvey Probber, Inc. demonstrates how individual systems can adapt to provide integration with modern technology.

also have some acoustic value; storage elements, ranging from simple shelves to massive cabinets; and integral lighting and wiring. Some systems begin with panels on which work surfaces and storage units are hung, some begin with desk or storage units to which privacy screens are attached, and some are made up of complete "work-station units" which combine work surfaces, storage, and privacy elements into complete assemblies. The use of systems furniture has a tendency to limit the openness of open planning, replacing truly open areas with clusters of screened units that often seem to approach the cubicles of a partitioned office. An excessive use of screen enclosure is probably the most common mistake in current open planning.

Even when an "open" plan seems to be drifting toward total enclosure, it still retains the virtues of easy flexibility, a flexibility that no conventionally partitioned office space can approach. The functional value of this flexibility and its economic concomitants are probably the most significant factors in the increasing acceptance of open planning in current practice.

The dominant trend in office design is toward *more* use of open planning. More than half of the office space currently being planned and constructed is said to be, in some way or other, "open" although an exact measure is hard to establish. Another trend, toward development of systems that are less rigid in dedication to either open or conventional planning

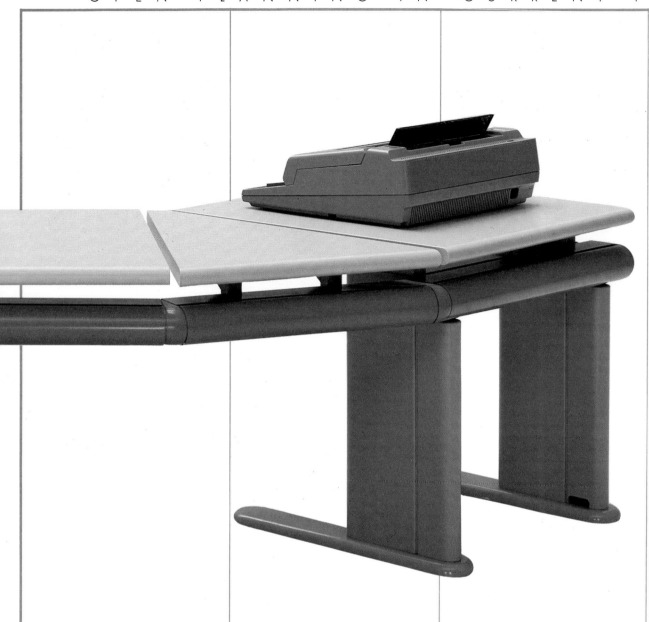

directions, includes panel or partition elements making possible enclosed rooms—even rooms with doors. Such systems offer compatibility and interchangeability of elements between open and partitioned space and make possible conversion of space from one planning approach to the other with a minimum of dislocation.

Planning is also responsive to the pressures of the electronic and computer revolution. The CRT (cathode ray tube) unit and the VDT (video display terminal) are everywhere and the minicomputer threatens to become as commonplace as the typewriter. Word processing, micrographics, teleconferencing are all techniques that have hardly had time to demonstrate their impact on office work and the facilities that house that work. The flexibility of open planning, and the equipment that has been developed to serve it, make it the preferred planning vocabulary in relation to all of these developing realities. Wiring may be made obsolete, perhaps, by fiber-optics, infrared, and radio communication. What constitutes good lighting and acoustics for an office is a matter for day-by-day study, debate, and revision.

In a scene in such rapid flux, the idea of openness, not just in terms of physical space, but in terms of ideas, concepts, and ways of thinking seems to have become essential. The open office is clearly here to stay and demands only the best, the most thoughtful, and the most flexible thinking to make it maximally useful.

A Survey of Office Furniture Systems

Although the originators of open plan (landscape) approaches were convinced that *any* tables and screens would serve the open plan concept effectively, subsequent developments have shown that special furniture for the open plan project can have major advantages. It *is* possible to use conventional desks, tables, chairs, and files in open layouts, and existing furniture can serve well where economy suggests avoiding purchase of new equipment. Still, it cannot be denied that systems developed specifically to serve open planning can have significant advantages.

The idea of a furniture "system" is based on the conviction that screen panels and work and storage components, if planned in an integrated way, can lead to workplaces that are both more efficient and more economical than anything that can be managed with unrelated desks, chairs, and screens. The office system thus emerges as a range of components that can be put together in a great variety of ways to serve all, or most, of the needs of a complete office project. The advantages include visual consistency that can give some order to the "scramble" of the landscape plan, the possibility of endless flexibility through regrouping of system elements, and when a system offers a full range of modern elements, highly

sophisticated ways to deal with problems of lighting, wiring, and accommodation of the "electronic office" elements.

Each system has a certain character of its own—there are always options to permit the planner to make a particular project unique; still, the system chosen establishes project style. Will the office be active, busy, quiet, serene? The system chosen may not determine this, but it sets limits and encourages certain directions.

Systems also have a tendency to "lock-in" the project, forcing loyalty to the system selected. It is possible, of course, to mix systems or to choose components from sources other than the dominant system supplier. Strong pressures, however, oppose such freedoms. Dedication to a particular system—all of whose components are fully interchangeable— furthers flexibility, one of the prime assets of open planning. Chairs from one source can be mixed with work stations from another with little problem, but mixing two or more panel- and work-station systems tends to be self-defeating.

A possible exception to this rule arises when a project is clearly divided into zones, each served by a system suited to the project area in question. This most often happens when a top executive area is identified and distinguished from a middle management or clerical area. This tends to make status distinctions clearly visible, for better or for worse, and also tends to limit the value of free interchange as a support to flexibility. A single system that can serve every area and every level has clear advantages. The manufacturers of systems know this and strive to capture projects from top to bottom by offering adaptable systems.

Once a system is chosen, the user organization must depend on the system manufacturer for replacements and extensions of the original project. A maker who drops a particular system or who goes out of business entirely leaves "orphans." Long-term stability, consistency, and a history of compatible, new products are of great importance in systems selection for use in large projects that have a long life expectancy.

Several hundred office systems are now in production. These cannot all be reviewed in any one compact book; however, the systems chosen for discussion here include several of the leading makers' products, several systems of unique character, and a range that suggests the variety of approaches available. Other systems not mentioned may be equally good or even better suited to a particular project. Such issues as availability at a particular location or on a particular

schedule may well take priority over all other values.

It is striking that systems can be classified into groups headed by a conceptual innovator and followed by a line of more-or-less imitative efforts. Imitations have a way of proving to be inferior to their models. One might expect that an imitator of an established product group would offer some improvements or economies. In practice, imitations never seem to make improvements (contrary to their claims), and where economies are offered, they are most often achieved through reductions in quality that are disproportionate to the promised gains. There are top-quality systems at various price levels, but bargain systems that mimic quality systems are rarely bargains.

Examinations of system installations and reports based on the experience over a period of time from system users are the best tests of system quality. Well-known manufacturers' systems with an extensive record of satisfactory use are not likely to be a disappointment. *Which* system will best suit a particular project is a matter of evaluation based on a careful comparison of the user's needs and the specifics that a particular system can best offer. The following pages illustrate a variety of manufacturers' systems.

Action Office System
HERMAN MILLER, INC.
Zeeland, Michigan

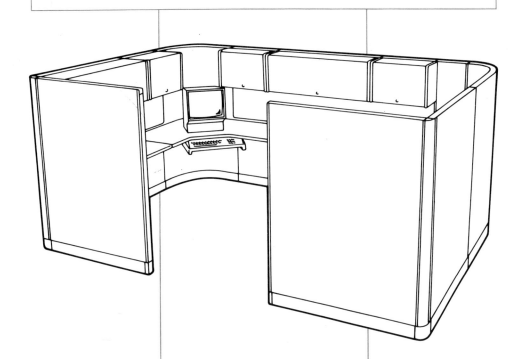

This system might be called the ancestor of all modern office systems. It developed, almost by accident, out of a research project undertaken by Robert Propst, who was seeking an improved setting for office work. The original "Action Office" included a collection of desk units, work tops, and storage components of a somewhat unconventional sort (a stand-up desk and the reintroduction of a rolltop, for example). When panels were added to support groupings of work tops and storage units, open planners seized on the system as an ideal way to provide flexibility, some degree of privacy without fixed walls, and ample storage tailored to the needs of the individual user. The manufacturer rapidly developed an extensive array of special components to suit every need including curved panels, glass panels, units for CRTs and other electronic components, accommodation for wiring and task-ambient lighting. An enclosed room and a compatible partitioning system provide a retreat from total openness.

This "prototypical panel system" (in which panels support all other components) has been widely imitated by other manufacturers. The imitations never seem to offer any improvements, and the original system is constantly updated to keep ahead of all competition.

Plans and photograph courtesy Herman Miller, Inc.

A sense of privacy and enclosed space is common in a typical work station like the one shown above.

This birdseye view displays a varied range of office arrangements and elements, including an enclosed room, glass panels, curved partitions, work tops, and storage components.

Elective Elements I (EE-I)

STOW/DAVIS: Grand Rapids, Michigan

The heart of this system is a special approach to the always troublesome problems of power supply and communications wiring management—problems constantly increasing as electronic office automation proliferates. The basic unit of EE-I is a steel structural frame that establishes the dimensions of a screen panel. Within this frame are full provisions for multiple wiring systems with vertical access for task and ambient lighting units, lateral connection to adjacent panels, and easy access to floor connections to outlets. A spacious wiring box may be attached to the frame at worktop level to form the rear of a top. Its lifttop and "brush" edge make it easy to bring wires to any piece of equipment at any point along the length of the wiring box.

Once wired up, the frame is hidden by snap-on face panels that can be removed at any time to permit changes and repairs to wiring with a minimum of disruption. Panel frames are near, but not at panel edges (connector brackets bridge the gap), so a hollow vertical space is also available for wiring wherever panels meet. Wires can be simply pushed in through the meeting point of the soft fabric panel edges. Tops, storage units, and files complete the system with a visual character that is quiet and conservative. This simple, elegant conservatism makes the sophisticated wiring provisions something of a surprise.

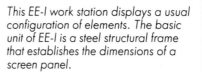
This EE-I work station displays a usual configuration of elements. The basic unit of EE-I is a steel structural frame that establishes the dimensions of a screen panel.

Photographs courtesy Stow/Davis

Showroom display set-ups hide the sophisticated wiring provisions, which facilitate electrical changes and repairs. The screen panels lift to reveal a hollow space for wiring.

Conference space is delineated in much the same way as individual work stations.

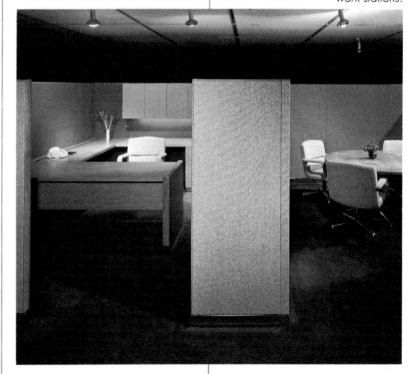

The work station at left is shared by two CRT users. Multiple wiring systems within the panels have vertical access for task lighting units and connection for the CRT units.

Haller System

HALLER SYSTEM, INC.
Irvine, California

This system, designed by Fritz Haller, a Swiss architect and design educator, has a distinct character unlike any other available product line. The heart of the system is a ball and screw connector that links slim chrome tubes to make modular cages. Any appropriate selection of shelves, panels, doors, drawers, bins, and accessories can go into the cages to make up individually tailored units for office work and storage needs. Large tops can be supported by tubular legs to make tables or, with the addition of storage and panel elements, desks in a full range of sizes and types. Casters can be added to provide mobile units. Screen panels and lighting accessories round out the list of elements needed for most open office needs.

In concept, the Haller system might be called "constructivist" in that it permits, even encourages, the planner to develop configurations from a kit of parts suggestive of Erector, Meccano, or Fisher Technik toys. The thin chrome tube edges of structure, the clear, bright, standard colors, and the modularity of the system give it a quality that might be called architectural. The system is indeed especially well liked by architects and architecturally oriented planners. Its flexibility is "total," since any unit can be reduced to fully interchangeable and reusable parts.

Slim chrome tubes that form modular cages characterize the Haller System in the reception and waiting area (above), general open work space (left), and executive work area with adjacent open conference/lounge space (below).

Icarus System

OLIVETTI SYNTHESIS S.P.A.
Milan, Italy

With Icarus, Olivetti steps into the production of a panel system while retaining the elements of a furniture system; that is, inclusion of desks and storage units that can stand free without panel attachment. Panels come in a range of heights and widths and are made of a four-sided metal frame that also serves as wiring duct, face panels, and edge-trim elements that complete the unit. Desks can have one or two slab legs of similar construction that also carry wiring. Alternative legs consist of a pedestal with twin, fat-tube legs. Desks can stand free or be connected in clusters. A range of storage components to hang on panels complements free-standing furniture-type storage units.

This system is clearly Olivetti's form of the panel system work station approach, similar to the earlier furniture-type Synthesis series. Design is by Sottsass and de Lucchi.

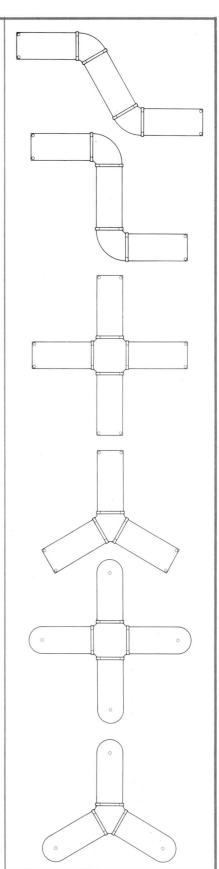

Six Icarus plan configurations show typical arrangements. Desks can stand free or be connected in clusters like these.

Drawing and photographs courtesy Olivetti Synthesis S.p.A.

The work station at left accommodates a CRT unit and printer with a minimum of exposed wiring. Locked storage is also provided.

A three-station cluster, with storage and screen elements, illustrates Olivetti's approach to panel systems.

Lucas Programmes 1 and 2

LUCAS FURNITURE SYSTEMS
London, England

These similar systems provide conventional-type desks and tables, screen panels and storage units, and possibilities for link-ups that lead to work stations with varied levels of enclosure. Programme 1, Lucas' first entry into the open plan office, uses a light, slim leg support for the typical work top. Programme 2 substitutes a larger leg element with solid vertical mass at the rear of each work top and with a somewhat heavier forward extending foot. Desk tops can include top-access file bins at the rear. Provisions for wiring, both for power and communications, are very complete, with wire ducts in screen panels and distribution channels at the rear of work tops.

Desks can be clustered in various configurations suitable to the more open forms of open planning, but the screens and storage components available can generate a "panel system" approach. Lucas' systems seem to have been developed to provide for a total range of needs from conventional, partitioned offices through screened work stations to totally open plans in the manner of the original office landscape concepts. The visual character is set by black metal supports, light wood surfaces, and bright, clear colors. The total effect is active and busy.

Lucas Programme systems can be used in a variety of settings, shown here in open space (left), in a minimal work station (right), and in two linked stations (below). The systems provide for a total range of needs, from conventional offices to open "landscape" plans.

Photographs by John Roaf, courtesy Lucas Furniture Systems

Marcatré System

ATELIER INTERNATIONAL, LTD.
New York, New York
and
MARCATRÉ S.P.A.: Misinto (Milan), Italy

This system, developed in Italy by Mario Bellini and first introduced in 1974, uses a limited number of basic furniture components to generate a range of tables, desks, complete work stations, and storage elements. It is not catalogued and distributed as separate components, but rather as a line of furniture units, each complete and self-contained even when the unit is a fairly complete work station incorporating work surfaces and surrounding panels to give a substantial level of privacy. There is, nevertheless, a high degree of flexibility through interchangeable parts.

Also, a limited range of large-scale "executive" desks and storage units clearly intended for use in conventional, partitioned offices complement related seating and lamps in this product group.

Although simple, rectangular-shaped units are a significant part of this system, its special character comes from the full availability of rounded form components. This includes an extensive range of conference tables, all either round or with half-circle rounded ends; work tops with semicircular ends; and a special top that extends a desk surface with a near three-quarter circle conference-area extension. Dominant finishes are natural wood and black, or as an alternative, white or beige.

Photographs courtesy Atelier International, Ltd.

Marcatré work stations in an open area (above) are complete and self-contained. At left, the work station's central element is the half-round, end work top. The characteristic three-quarter circle desk-end element provides a conference-area extension (right, above and below).

Race System

SUNAR
Norwalk, Connecticut
and
Waterloo, Ontario

The Race system cannot be classified as either a panel system or a work station system. Rather it uses a unique approach in which the electrical "race" that gives the system its name takes the form of horizontal bars supported by posts at ends and at regular intervals in longer runs. This creates a fence like structure on which work surfaces and storage components are hung. Upward extensions of the vertical support posts can hold padded panels that provide some visual and acoustic privacy and can also support additional storage elements and additional lighting.

The system is particularly suited to the most heavily "electronic" offices where wiring, repairs, and revisions to wiring are a constant problem. A Race installation tends to look more open and more active than most other office systems. The designer, Douglas Ball, had developed several other systems previously for the same manufacturer; these are closed in character compared to other office systems. The Race system rounds out this product group with one of the most flexible and "advanced" of currently available office furniture systems.

The Race System (left), in typical open groupings, tends to look more open and more active than other office systems. The "race" itself (above) defines boundaries of open work stations. Soft "pillow" elements (right) provide privacy enclosures above the raceway.

Stephens System

KNOLL INTERNATIONAL, INC.
New York, New York

The Stephens system had its origins in the open plan project for the headquarters of the Weyerhaeuser Company in Tacoma, Washington. The architects, Skidmore, Owings and Merrill, dissatisfied with any available office furniture at the time the building was being designed, asked Knoll International to undertake development of a new system tuned to the specific requirements of this project. Bill Stephens, the designer Knoll put in charge, developed this outstanding example of what has come to be called the work station approach to open plan furniture. The basic unit in any such system is not a panel or a desk, but an assembly that is a combined work surface, surrounding enclosure, and storage area. Stephens called this unit a "machine station" with the idea that it would most often accommodate a typewriter or some other piece of office equipment, perhaps even a computer.

There are also tables and desks, screen panels, and file enclosures to round out the system and make it usable in conventional offices as well as in open space. The primary surfaces are in natural wood finishes; tops and metal storage insert components come in white and neutral tones. Screen panels are offered with fabric surfaces. There is a certain quality of dignity about the Stephens system that comes from its proportions and finishes. The system itself gives a sense of solidity and permanence which sometimes is difficult to achieve with other systems.

An executive work station with adjacent informal conference area displays the dignity of the Stephens System.

The first important Stephens System installation was at the Weyerhauser headquarters in Tacoma, Washington.

Photograph courtesy Knoll International, Inc.

Steelcase 9000

STEELCASE, INC.
Grand Rapids, Michigan

Steelcase is the largest manufacturer of office furniture in the United States and has made a point of establishing a dominant position in furniture especially suited to open plan projects. As the company name implies, Steelcase is primarily a maker of steel furniture (with occasional wood components and finishes) with a reputation for quality engineering and super-sturdy construction. The 9000 system has its origins in time-tested details for steel desk construction— tops, drawers, file units with excellent quality structure, hardware, and details. In the 9000 series, these details merge into a system that includes panel elements to create work station assemblies and provide a full range of privacy options from conventional desks for bullpen use to virtually complete private offices.

A solid down-to-the-floor mass, with rounded edge details (that may be chrome or one of several neutral color metal finishes), gives to the 9000 a look of weight and strength. The system is, nevertheless, fully demountable and flexible through full interchangeability of parts.

Provisions for concealed power and communications wiring are very complete, and lighting and storage accessories are available in great variety. Seating, tables, and files from the full Steelcase product line fill out a roster of elements available from this single source.

Photographs courtesy Steelcase, Inc.

The 45°-angle work top extends the desk's functions; the larger area creates a conference area for small meetings.

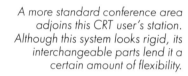

A more standard conference area adjoins this CRT user's station. Although this system looks rigid, its interchangeable parts lend it a certain amount of flexibility.

Straight and curved, glazed panels in the 9000 system groupings allow light to enter the office while still maintaining some privacy.

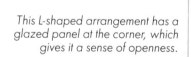

This L-shaped arrangement has a glazed panel at the corner, which gives it a sense of openness.

These compact work stations for CRT users have provisions for concealed power and communications wiring.

Synthesis Systems 45, 45CR and 80

OLIVETTI: Milan, Italy

In this closely related group of systems, the designers, Ettore Sottsass, Jr. and (in the case of Series 45CR) Michele de Lucchi, have stayed closer to the intentions of the originators of office landscape than have the designers of many recent systems. The basic components are desks that are really tables with separable pedestals, roll-around file units, and storage units of several types, all self-contained pieces of furniture quite as useful in a conventionally partitioned office as in open plan areas. To adapt for use in open planning, screen panels—flat planes hinged together—stand up dependent on a corner or zig-zag arrangement. The 45CR series can also be adapted for cluster groupings with corner connector tops that generate various configurations. Wiring channel accessories, special tables for VDTs and printers are available, making this group particularly suitable to offices with a high proportion of electronically equipped work stations.

Series 80 differs most obviously from series 45 in its more sober colors, wood finishes, and similar appearance variants suggesting an intention to provide visible elements for status differentiation. Many accessory components are common to both series. The aesthetic is bright, lively, and in a subtle way, it is very Italian.

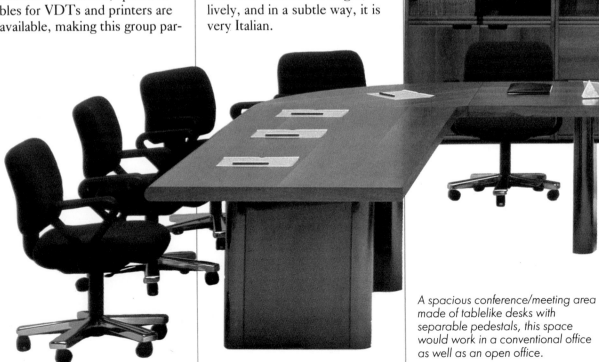

A spacious conference/meeting area made of tablelike desks with separable pedestals, this space would work in a conventional office as well as an open office.

The details of these systems—wire access (above left and center), file inserts (above right), and typical rounded edges (above)—make this group visually interesting and particularly suited to electronically oriented offices.

Photographs courtesy Olivetti Synthesis S.p.A.

Voice System

PLUS COMPANY, LTD.
Tokyo, Japan

Offices of modern Japanese corporations tend to continue the crowded and messy characteristics of the "American plan" bullpen of the 1920s and '30s. A new awareness of more thoughtfully planned offices has now surfaced in Japan along with a concern for office aesthetics that relates to traditional Japanese thinking about architecture and residential interior design. At the same time, the Japanese emphasis on group or team work patterns has encouraged a special approach to office systems based on the assumption that most office personnel will be part of a group. Most groups average from five to seven workers, who must all be in constant visual contact and constant auditory contact.

The Voice system gets its name from its concern for providing spoken communication between the members of a group while offering generally acceptable acoustical control. Screens are made up of an internal frame plus applied surface panels. Wiring travels within the hollow space defined by the frame. Panels are divided horizontally into sections making various heights available for varied degrees of separation and contact between users. There are window panels with integral blinds for changeable open vision or privacy at a moment's notice and a full range of lighting and other accessories. Standard colors are unusually bright and strong (by Western standards) and outstandingly attractive.

Voice groupings in strong reds and greens are bright and outstanding. Note the different heights among the dividers and the plant, both of which add visual interest to the set-up. The system fits into the Japanese pattern of providing space for work teams as opposed to individuals.

Photographs by Nihon Hasshoku, drawing and photographs courtesy Plus Co., Ltd.

VOKO M.E.P./R. Typ 1, 2, and 3

VOKO—FRANZ VOGT AND CO.
Giessen, West Germany

VOKO is one of the leading European office furniture manufacturers and a dominant force in setting the character of open plan furniture in European markets. The VOKO systems offer a range of products from free-standing desks and tables through screen elements to fully integrated open plan systems in which storage and work top elements are tied into panels to produce integrated work stations. VOKO components are solid, boxy, modular, and organized in a way that seems to recall roots stretching back to Bauhaus design thinking.

Desk support structures can be inverted U's of fairly light profile, C's with a long forward cantilever, or C's with a massive rear vertical and stubby forward cantilever. Electrical wire ducting is standard, and all edges and corners are well rounded in accordance with modern German practice. Work station components with full adjustability to accommodate electronic office devices (VDTs, CRTs etc.) are provided, and a related system of full height (to the ceiling) panel and storage components is available for those who wish to retreat from the open.

Curved panels, tops, and shelves encourage characteristic VOKO clusters with rounded ends and serpentine configurations. Work stations can accommodate modern technological equipment as well as standard office supplies.

Photographs by Gie Ben, courtesy Voko-Franz Vogt and Co.

Zapf System

KNOLL INTERNATIONAL, INC.
New York, New York

Otto Zapf was asked to develop an office system closely paralleling and compatible with the Stephens system but lighter in character and scale. The Zapf system is, like Stephens, a work station system in which the basic planning unit is a work surface set in a surrounding of panels. Extensions, storage units, additional panels, task lighting, and special components for office automation equipment round out the system and make it usable in many applications.

The visual character of Zapf centers around the typical fabric-covered panel and slim, rounded, vertical edges. Available fabrics include a range of soft and subtle colors which give work stations a quiet and humane atmosphere that seems special to Zapf installations.

Complete work stations can be moved, even loaded, with users' papers and equipment without disassembly—an aid to flexibility. A special dolly is provided so work stations can be wheeled to a new location as easily as a file cabinet.

There is a complete range of power and communications wiring accessories and a full range of special-purpose elements including glazed panels, curved panels (fabric or glazed), and even an adjustable rollaround stand for VDT unit support.

This Zapf System is in use in Knoll's own design center, where existing cast-iron classic columns provide an amusing foil. (For further detail, refer to the floor plan on page 68.)

Photographs courtesy Knoll International, Inc.

Analysis of Costs

In any discussion of a proposed office planning project, the question arises: "What is all this going to cost?" When open planning is under consideration, especially if it is being compared with conventional planning, relative cost becomes a major topic. Unfortunately, we live in a period of constantly rising costs, so any discussion of specific figures is destined to go out of date within months. *Relative* costs, however, remain fairly consistent, and it is certainly possible to review the ways in which specific cost comparisons can be set up.

Office renovation, relocation, or the establishment of a new office will generate costs that are not particularly welcome. It would be "cheaper" to stay in the old place, get along as we are doing now, or otherwise evade spending money on a new or improved facility. A new factory, a new store, can be seen as an investment leading to immediate profits. A new office is not, in most situations, so directly related to any specific financial gains. These realities often lead to an excessively "cheeseparing" psychology in which every penny spent is viewed as a luxury expenditure or even as an out-of-pocket loss. A more reasonable view must begin with acceptance of the reality that the office exists for genuine purposes and that the specifics of the office facility must further those purposes. For profit-making business, this means that the office contributes to the firm's financial success; for nonprofit organizations, the office exists to accomplish the organization's purposes as efficiently and effectively as possible. To evaluate office performance in these terms, it is necessary to look at *all* of the costs associated with the office's functions over its useful life.

Preparing this evaluation will immediately make it clear that staff salary and salary-related costs are by far the largest items and that the cost of setting up and operating the physical facility will usually represent no more than five to ten percent of the total. Anything that will make the office users' performance more effective, that will, to use a favorite modern term, improve *productivity* in any significant way, will surely be worthwhile. Unfortunately, clear measures of productivity in office work are hard to come by. Some recent studies[1] suggest that there is a measurable improvement in productivity in a "better" office environment, but making a specific estimate of what improvement to anticipate in a particular new facility while it is still in the planning stage remains difficult or impossible. Attention, therefore, moves to the specifics of initial costs of a new installation and its operational costs over its life cycle. In looking at such comparisons, it is important to remember how insignificant these items are in relation to the total cost (including salaries) that the office will represent over the years.

It is also common to overemphasize the significance of initial costs. This is, of course, money that must be found and spent before the new office even begins operations, but, if one assumes a ten- to twenty-year useful life (and there are many offices operating for thirty, forty, or even fifty years), costs of operation, maintenance, and renovation pull ahead of first cost in importance. Still, when open planning is up for consideration, it is the *comparative cost* that comes into question. There is no general answer. Instead, one must set up a comparison between a specific, proposed open plan facility and an alternative. The alternative might be the existing office, a luxurious conventional office, a spartan conventional office,

or a conventional office roughly comparable to the proposed open office in standards of quality. This latter case, the comparison most often sought, generates a common expectation that the open plan project will save money. Certainly, an open plan proposal can be *made* to save money, but this is not necessarily wise if some of the merits of open planning are canceled out as a result.

The expectation of saving comes, obviously, from the omission of partitioning. No walls are bound to be less costly than some walls. There can also be related savings in the first costs, from simplifications in air-conditioning and heat arrangements, in lighting, and other lesser items. The other anticipated cost-reduction results from the possibility of reducing the total floor area of a project. Each of these possible savings must be viewed with caution if one is to arrive at a fully satisfactory open project. Savings from the elimination of walls and doors will usually be offset by the cost of furniture systems including screen panels and with such extras as the ubiquitous plants that are commonly found in a landscape project. In a partitioned private office, a desk and a few chairs, perhaps a file or credenza, will serve user needs; possibly old furniture can be reused. In an open office, a "system" work station is likely to be more complex and much more expensive, particularly if panels are provided to build up privacy and if generous storage is included. If the plan involves saving money by "compacting" to reduce floor area, a sense of crowding may develop with related acoustical problems and a resultant loss in the hoped-for improved flexibility of layout.

The open office also demands carpeting throughout (now usually provided in conventional offices also) and may require additional acoustical treatment and equipment. The need for extra "quiet rooms" or phone enclosures, lounges and similar

[1]A particularly interesting study, *The Impact of Office Environment on Productivity and Quality of Working Life* by BOSTI (Buffalo Organization for Social and Technological Innovation) is due out in 1984, but a survey of findings is available now from Steelcase, Inc. in Grand Rapids, Michigan.

"extras" may also eat away the savings in wall construction.

These considerations add up to a general opinion on the part of planners that open planning cannot, or should not, be used to save on the initial costs. By good fortune or clever planning, some savings may be found, but not even the best planner should not expect to save more than five or ten percent. The real financial gains in open planning show up over a life cycle that includes estimated maintenance costs and the expense of changes and renovations. Unfortunately, since these are *future* costs, firm figures cannot be developed; estimates must be made carefully to ensure that they are not slanted to benefit one proposal or another. Reduction in maintenance costs comes from the greater ease of cleaning open space as compared to moving in and out of private rooms and cubicles. The only increase in maintenance comes from plant care and replacement. In general, maintenance costs of open offices can save anywhere from 10 to 50 percent over those of conventional offices.

Ease in making layout changes is a more difficult factor to evaluate. An open plan work station can be knocked down and relocated very quickly and without specialized or skilled labor. Electrical and phone changes related to replanning are also generally easier in open plan offices, although different systems vary in this respect. In comparison, tearing down and rebuilding a partitioned office is slow, messy, and costly. Changes in lighting, air-conditioning, and floor covering in the conventional office add to the costs and often discourage making changes that are really needed. It is certainly clear that each layout change that will be made over an office's life will show up as highly favorable to open plan. The difficulty is in estimating how many such changes will be needed and how extensive they will be. Past experience is the best guide, although allowance should be made for changes needed but never made because of the inflexibility of conventional planning.

To add to these uncertainties, note that the basis on which the office space is occupied (owned or rented) and how the original installation will be financed must be taken into account. In rental space, the building owner will often provide partitioning, lighting, and floor covering under terms of the lease. Omitting or changing the "building standard" may not lead to credits that really reflect the actual savings of open planning. The status of walls versus furniture in terms of tax treatment can also be a factor in the total cost impact of one planning system versus another. Finally, the great intangible is an estimate of the increased productivity that the new office promises. In spite of favorable predictions for open plan facilities, a specific estimate of what can be expected from a particular project is really impossible to produce. Most cost comparisons leave this matter out of the figures and simply refer to it as a hoped-for but imponderable gain.

In spite of the difficulties in arriving at precise estimates of relative costs, it is still possible, with all the issues discussed above in mind, to set up a comparison that will give a fairly clear idea of what the impact of open planning will be for a specific office facility. The first step in doing this is to select (or assume) a specific space with a known rental or construction cost. Preliminary plans can then be developed in conventional and open planning modes in sufficient detail to provide data for use in the comparison schedule outlined below. Combinations of open and conventional planning can, of course, also be considered. The preliminary plans should be sufficiently specific to make possible an estimate of the impact of open planning on total floor area requirements. Assuming equal area for both systems is almost always safe, a saving of 10 percent for open planning is conservative. Any attempt at an area saving greater than this should be viewed with caution. Next, sources must be found for current estimates on construction and purchase costs of various items at the time and place where the facility will be built. Architects, office planners, and contractors with active experience in office construction are the sources of these figures. Even though overly optimistic figures are sometimes provided by such sources, the *relative* cost levels that are derived should prove reliable. Furniture costs can also be obtained from probable suppliers of the furniture to be used. See also a detailed note relating to the schedule below. To use the schedule, the following figures will be needed:

Rental cost or construction cost of basic space per sq. ft. _____
Allowance for floor covering per sq. ft. _____[1]
Allowance for ceiling treatment per sq. ft. _____[1]
Allowance for lighting per sq. ft. _____[1]
Allowance for HVAC installation per sq. ft. _____[1]
Budget for cleaning and maintenance per sq. ft. _____[1]
Allowance in watts per sq. ft. for lighting _____[1]
Allowance in watts per sq. ft. for HVAC _____[1]
Cost of fixed partitioning per linear foot _____
Cost of movable partitioning per linear foot _____
Cost of typical door and buck (frame) _____
Cost of electrical power per KWH _____[2]

[1]For each of these items, obtain two estimates; one applicable to conventional, one to open planning.

[2]It would be desirable to have estimates for this figure reflecting probable change (increase) over the life of the facility, but there is no certain way to make such a projection. The local utility's best guess will have to serve.

It is now possible to make up comparative cost schedules presenting estimated first cost and annual cost in something similar to the following format:

FIRST COST	CONVENTIONAL	OPEN PLAN
Fixed partitioning _____ ft.@ _____	_____	_____
Movable partitioning _____ ft.@ _____	_____	_____
Doors _____ @ _____	_____	_____
Floor covering[1]	_____	_____
Ceiling treatment[1]	_____	_____
Window treatment[1]	_____	_____
Lighting[1]	_____	_____
HVAC	_____	_____
Furniture		
_____ Exec. work stations[2]	_____	_____
_____ Mid. Man. work stations[2]	_____	_____
_____ Clerical work stations[2]	_____	_____
Conference	_____	_____
Reception	_____	_____
Filing & storage	_____	_____
Other	_____	_____
Plants and accessories	_____	_____
Special provisions:		
Quiet rooms	_____	_____
Telephone	_____	_____
Other	_____	_____
Acoustical system[3]	_____	_____

Notes:

[1]Use different sq. ft. figure and adjusted total floor area figure in each column.

[2]For best accuracy, make a specific furniture selection for typical stations at the three levels suggested for each planning system. In open planning, where panels or screens are shared, use only the appropriate percentage of the cost of shared elements.

[3]This item is normally required for open plan installations only.

ANNUAL COST	CONVENTIONAL	OPEN PLAN
Rent or amortization of construction cost (basic "raw" space)	_____	_____
Amortization of "First Cost" items listed above[1]	_____	_____
Utilities: _____ KWH@ _____	_____	_____
Maintenance (cleaning and repairs)	_____	_____
Replacements[2]	_____	_____
Relocation and renovation of _____ work stations@ _____[3]	_____	_____
Other	_____	_____
Adjustments to reflect impact on taxation and other financial factors	_____	_____

Notes:

[1]Note that different time periods are applicable to items with different useful life. Some items (furniture, for example) may still have cash value at the end of a useful life in this facility, which should be allowed for.

[2]This item refers to anticipated replacement of carpets, upholstery, plants, and accessories that require routine replacement.

[3]This item is normally required for open plan installations only.

Totals derived from both schedules will give a reliable picture of the financial impact of use of open planning, and if the data used are accurate, a reasonably accurate sense of actual cost of the facility being planned. It is inevitable that the actual life of an office facility is difficult to predict. Unforeseen events may lead to relocation or shut-down much earlier than expected, while a well-planned and adaptable office may remain in service many more years than might be predicted. It may be helpful, then, to make the annual cost estimate on a range of lifespan periods ranging from very short to much longer than normal. Results can be displayed graphically to make the impact of possible lifespans clearly visible.

Finally, in order to develop a genuine perspective on the significance of expenses, facility costs should always be looked at in relation to *total* office operational costs, including salaries, equipment, supplies, etc. A graphic display of this relationship is also helpful in developing a sense of the financial impact of planning decisions.

Case Studies

The selection of a few case studies for closer examination has not been easy. There must now be thousands of open office installations scattered over the globe. Quality and success are not always easy to assess on the basis of the glamorous photographs and verbal reports that come back from every project. The case studies selected for inclusion here represent a wide range of projects from very large to quite small, from totally "landscape" to rather conventionally cautious explorations of open plan concepts. They were also chosen to provide a wide international range of office planning concepts and to show what happens in the full spectrum from a new-building project to planning within older structures and "adaptive reuse."

There is no substitute for actually visiting projects. In reality, some projects that seem quite routine in pictures turn out to have a surprising vitality and life. Projects that photograph well are sometimes less successful in terms of daily use than their visual images would suggest. The open projects illustrated here have each, in their own way, demonstrated the possibilities for success in office planning based on open concepts.

Probably the most interesting generalization that can be extracted from a survey of this group of projects has to do with its variety. Complaints against open planning have often centered on its supposed uniformity. "All open offices look exactly alike," critics have complained. Each office system is accused of asserting a uniform character that will be the inevitable result of using that system in any space. There may be a shred of truth in this, but the extreme variety in the projects illustrated here suggests that, in the hands of skillful designers and planners, open offices need not adhere to uniform patterns.

Stories of user dissatisfaction with open planning continue to be heard, and some planners discuss a "backlash" reaction toward privacy, partitions, and cubicles. On site, at the projects included here, one does not hear these protests. The visitor is generally surprised by the overall sense of quiet, serenity, and order. Users, chosen at random and asked about their reactions on the basis of daily experience, tend to be either euphorically favorable or almost unaware that the place in which they are working is in any way special.

The best of open offices can seem quite utopian, in fact. Visitors from far away, who come to study offices that have developed an international reputation, leave as "converts," convinced that this way of dealing with office space comes close to real organizational needs and to individual human needs than any other identifiable approach. Modern organizations, with their vastness and their all-too-automated ways of dealing with individual people, represent a large-scale social problem that converts into problems for individuals.

The physical environment of the workplace is only one factor in the work experience, and not, perhaps, the most important factor. The environmental factor may well be least important at the top management levels (the very levels where the environment is most likely to be of high quality). At the lower end of the hierarchy where more routine work is increasingly a matter of machine interface, the environment becomes the most dominating aspect of the work experience. If one-third of a person's life is to be spent in an office, what that office is like becomes a significant aspect of general life experience. Is it best spent in a boxlike cubicle or in a partitioned space set out with status trappings such as credenzas and Thermos jugs? The reader is urged to make visits—direct experience is the only really trustworthy test.

J. A. Alstrup A/S
OFFICE BUILDING

Hasselager, Denmark
Knud Blach Petersen, architects

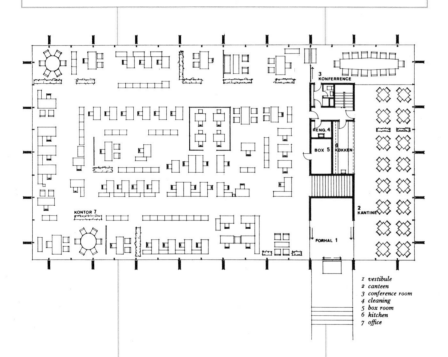

3 KONFERRENCE

RENG. 4

BOX 5   6 KØKKEN

2 KANTINE

KONTOR 7

FORHAL 1

1 vestibule
2 canteen
3 conference room
4 cleaning
5 box room
6 kitchen
7 office

A small office building on a rural site provides the general offices for a glass wholesale distributor adjacent to a larger warehouse and factory block. Conceptually, the building consists of a single-floor platform with glass perimeter walls and a roof grid supported by columns that extend outward from the glass walls. The roof grid is a concrete structure that extends upward from the building walls to form a sun screen and that also screens the skylights in the actual roof.

Internally, about three-fourths of the building is one large open office space with about sixty workplaces—executive, managerial, and clerical—all fully open with only screens and plant boxes providing spatial division. The remainder of the building contains enclosed spaces for a reception area, conference room, employee cafeteria, and a service area.

Daylight, coming from the roof skylights, is a primary source of illumination throughout the office space; in addition, each skylight square is surrounded by a square of fluorescent fixtures so that artificial light (for dark days and late hours) will come from the same general direction as daylight. A tunnel connects the office building with the nearby factory warehouse making bad-weather communication easy.

Drawing and photographs by Thomas Pedersen OG Poul Pedersen, courtesy Knud Blach Petersen Architects

The building exterior shows the overhang of the concrete roof grid that extends up from the roof, which is about three feet below.

This open executive area leads to the conference room beyond, which can be seen through the glass wall. This system fits in well with the light and greenery of the office space.

AT&T Long Lines

EASTERN REGIONAL HEADQUARTERS

Oakton, Virginia
Kohn Pedersen Fox Associates P.C., architects and interior designers with dePolo/Dunbar

Bridges cross through the galleria space, making a dramatic and unusual statement.

Sixteen hundred workers are accommodated here in a 400,000 sq. ft. building cluster on a 34-acre suburban site. There are three floors of office space in four "pods," three blocks of open office space, and a fourth quadrant-shaped unit for executive offices, a cafeteria, and auditorium. To give variety and focus to the general office space, there is a galleria over three hundred feet long and four stories high forming a kind of internal "main street." Bridges cross through it at each floor level and an "atrium" extension branches off; lounges occur at the upper floor levels at each end. The Crystal Palace-like spaces form a dramatic change in scale as compared to the general office working spaces.

The executive offices are conventionally partitioned, but the remainder of the working space is open plan. Rather than accepting a standard furniture system, Jack Dunbar (in charge of interior planning) developed a custom system using simple, shelf worktops supported on standard file and storage units.

Custom-built screen-enclosure panels in a natural wood finish define work stations with a surrounding "wall" that is high enough to screen work tops but low enough to permit visual contact and conversational contact with adjacent stations. The modular design of the system here makes rearrangement easy and flexible.

Although the executive offices are conventionally partitioned, the reception area stands out with its large circular skylight.

Lounge spaces on both levels complement the light, airy space of the galleria.

The general office space uses simple, open work stations made from standard file units with custom tops and dividers.

BEA Offices

New York, New York
Tod Williams and Associates, architects

This 16,000-sq.-ft. office, a bit more than half of a high floor in the Citicorp tower, provides work space for a staff of about thirty who make up a financial investment firm. The planning concept establishes a delicate balance between openness and a provision for considerable privacy for managers. There *are* private offices, but they are also open, in the sense that walls are screening enclosures and do not extend to the ceiling. Privacy comes from a generous assignment of space and from planning that makes secretarial areas something of a barrier zone, screening the inner offices.

The secretarial areas and most of the remaining work space is fully open, although work stations are designed to create a strong feeling of personal territory. Files and storage occupy an enclosed zone, and the end corners of the L-shaped plan are assigned to a fully enclosed lounge at one end and a similar conference room at the other. Even these spaces share a sense of openness since their walls are glass with a pattern of sand-blasted ("frosted") squares; the clear bands between the obscured areas permit a see-through glimpse. A small library occupies a drum-shaped block, which is also open, but with its floor up a step so as to give a sense of separation from the general floor area.

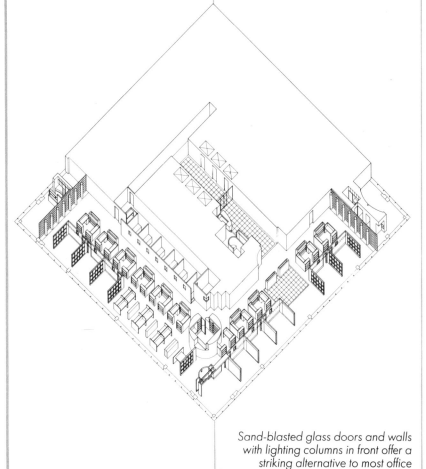

Sand-blasted glass doors and walls with lighting columns in front offer a striking alternative to most office interiors.

Photographs © Norman McGrath, plan and photographs courtesy Tod Williams and Associates

Electronic work stations and lines of files or storage cabinets define the perimeter office areas (right). These open plan areas have a raised floor and exposed ceiling (below).

A. G. Becker, Inc.

New York, New York
Jack L. Gordon, architects

Four floors of about 70,000 sq. ft. in an older office building were remodeled to accommodate some five hundred people in a securities firm in New York's Wall Street area. The planners had to contend with a heavy concentration of electronic equipment and a serious problem of security and control here. The building's central core has been treated as a permanent, "hard" area (an area that can't be changed, such as elevators and stairwells) with a general reception control point at one end, and a special counter and waiting area at the other end to deal with the heavy messenger traffic that the firm's work requires. Most of the building's perimeter is devoted to open plan areas with a six-inch raised access floor to permit easy wiring distribution. To avoid a low ceiling throughout the space (created by existing structure and the raised floor), it was decided to omit a hung, flush ceiling in the perimeter zone. Instead, beams and air-conditioning ducts are exposed with lighting laid out in a regular pattern fitted within the grid of structure and ducts.

The added sense of height results in a feeling of light and view within the entire space. Although work areas are open, departments and subunits are defined by lines of files or storage cabinets, or by screen panels which are part of the Steelcase 9000 furniture system.

Photographs courtesy Jack L. Gordon

Semiprivate work stations (right) and a private corner office (below) illustrate the use of glass walls and partitions.

Centraal Beheer

Apeldoorn, Holland
Herman Hertzberger, architect

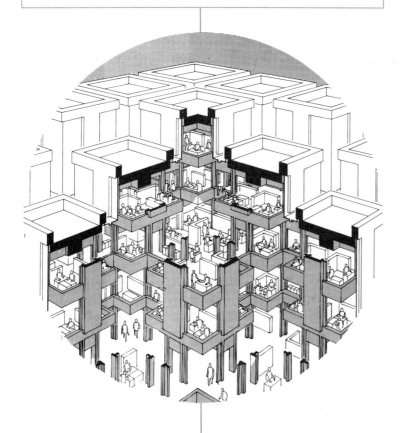

The Centraal Beheer building remains one of the most startling of all open office projects. The architect's concern with the building as a humane workplace led to a decision to forego vast open floors and substitute a concept in which small (9 x 9 meter) modules are clustered in a grid looking out over open shared space which extends up through the building's four main levels. Each module connects to its neighbors by bridges; its four corners become balconies overlooking the open interior space. The purpose is to escape the monotony of vast floors of endless work stations and to substitute small work areas in which each working group can establish a more personal identity.

To give a further sense of individualization, there is no standard furniture layout or interior design concept imposed throughout the building. Instead, individual employees are encouraged to arrange furniture as they choose, to add plants, accessories, and decorative details, even lighting. This may seem a recipe for chaos, and it is certainly true that many office planners would be disturbed by the almost random way in which the work spaces turn out. The forms of the building structure are, however, very strong and set a dominating character for the interior that seems to absorb the confusion of "personalization" very effectively.

Vertical circulation is at the center of the building mass and leads to reception points on each floor. Conference areas and coffee bars are clustered near the center. A restaurant, a nursery, and a roof terrace help increase the individual employee's sense of group identity.

The "hanging gardens" of these work areas are typical of this project, which strives to be a humane workplace.

Channing L. Bete Co.
CORPORATE HEADQUARTERS

South Deerfield, Massachusetts
Juster Pope Associates, architects

This building houses the operations of a small corporation that plans, designs, and produces publications with a wide distribution. Standing in a cold climate, the building has been planned to maximize advantages available from solar energy. It houses a printing plant along with the offices that generate the material to be printed. The office portion of the building includes executive and managerial offices that lean toward the conventional. Reception, conference, and cafeteria spaces are standard, while open general offices hint at an awareness of Bürolandschaft concepts. The most open portions of the total office installation are, of course, most flexible.

Rearrangement of work groups is simple and easy in space that is free of any fixed architectural elements. Managerial concerns for privacy and status identification have been met without any sharp distinctions between "officers" and "troops."

A larger, glass-walled conference room leans toward conventional office-plan practices.

A typical work area (left) hints at an awareness of Burolandschaft concepts. The small conference room (above), off the reception area, is shared space for the entire office.

Photographs by D. Randolph Foulds, courtesy Juster Pope Associates

John Deere and Company
WEST OFFICE BUILDING

Moline, Illinois
Kevin Roche, John Dinkeloo, and Associates, architects

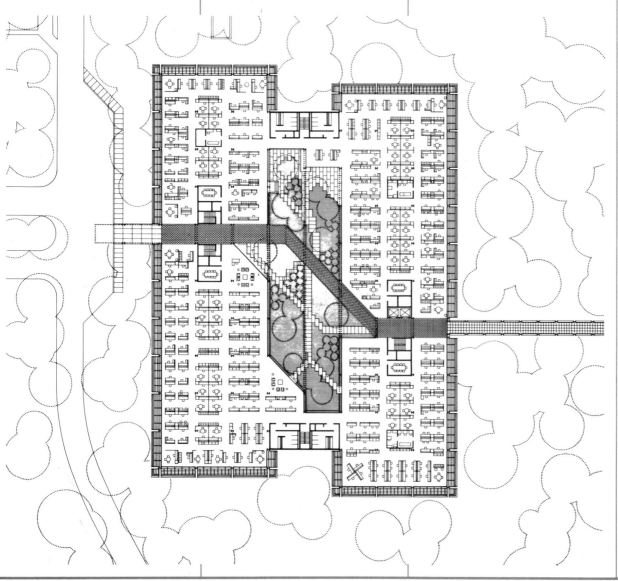

Plan courtesy John Pile

The John Deere corporate headquarters, a well-known project of the office of Eero Saarinen in the late 1950s, is built in an extensive, parklike setting with offices arranged in a conventional, partitioned fashion. The new, west building, connected to the older building by a bridge passage, is a more spread out, two-story block made of two rectangles connected by a central garden atrium. Each rectangle has a central "spine" occupied by service areas, conference rooms, and the semi-enclosed offices of managers. The remaining space is occupied by open work stations, all within view of either an exterior window wall or the internal garden.

Work stations are in orderly, geometric rows and are screened with low, enclosing panels. There is considerable variety in work station layout, but a sense of orderliness and pattern prevails nevertheless. The central, skylit garden is the focus of the building, and the office spaces resemble terraces overlooking the garden in a way that makes the whole building interior into one unified space.

Geometric rows of work stations line a terracelike circulation gallery (right) and the central garden atrium (below), which is the focus of the building.

Dial Financial Corp.

Des Moines, Iowa
John Pile, office planning and interior design

A reception area near the executive office highlights paintings from the corporate art collection.

Originally a parking garage, this older building had served the firm as corporate headquarters but had declined into a rabbit-warren of unworkable spaces. A general planning analysis developed a totally new approach to space allocations. The decision to take the open plan route made all of the working space fully flexible.

Some clerical areas are open in bullpen fashion with desks lined up in rows, but a major part of the facility is devoted to screened work stations. These work stations are open but still somewhat private, for the use of computer programmers and other semiprofessional office workers.

Needs for total privacy are met with conference rooms of various sizes and with the provision of "quiet rooms," small cubicles with seating, writing desks, and telephones, available to anyone who needs quiet for work related or private phoning, study, or writing, or for the sorts of conversations that cannot take place in totally un-screened open space.

Executive quarters are fully open, more spacious than other areas, and somewhat screened by secretarial areas, but still not sealed off from general work spaces.

A private "quiet room" (above) is for use as needed, while the open, clerical area resembles the bullpens of early offices.

Knoll International, Inc.
DESIGN CENTER

New York, New York
Paul Haigh, architecture and design

Knoll is a leading manufacturer of office furniture systems and a leading presence in production of the whole range of furniture products that are the standard bearers of the modern movement. A certain dissatisfaction with the cramped spaces of New York office buildings led to a decision to acquire generous floor space in a loft building in the increasingly prestigious area of SoHo. A large, older loft building has been renovated as a "design center" to house Knoll activities that have to do with new product development and all the other design-oriented work that is part of Knoll.

The high ceilings and cast-iron columns that are basic parts of the building have been preserved, and such new elements as spiral stairs to connect floors and tubular ducts for air-conditioning have been inserted. The resulting interior spaces have been outfitted with Knoll systems furniture—the Zapf system, in particular—that demonstrates the daily use of open planning.

Color is used in particularly subtle ways. The systems furniture is austere and neutral in tone, while sharp colors—acid greens, for example—appear in thin edges. The effect is spacious and lively.

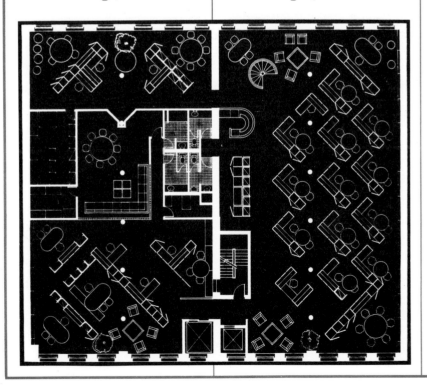

An open work area in a loft space is complemented by a spiral staircase. Color is used especially well in the systems furniture here, with the sharper hues appearing in the thin edges of architectural elements.

Photograph by Bo Parker, plan and photograph courtesy Haigh Architecture

Merck Sharp & Dohme

HEADQUARTERS BUILDING

West Point, Pennsylvania
MBA Associates and Planners, architects
ISD with MBA, interior designers

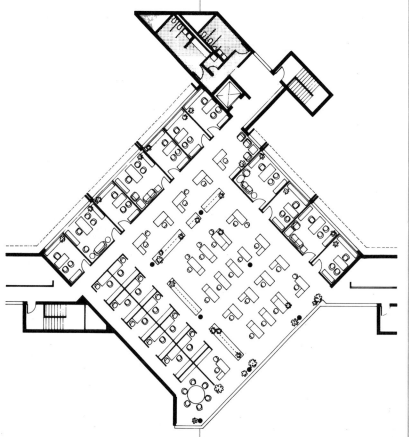

Window light and a view of the outside are available to all the workers using these CRTs in the open "pool" area of the office.

This 120,000-sq.-ft. cluster, the winning design of an architectural competition, is connected to preexisting buildings on the site by a circulation "spine." Attached to the spine are three similar square office blocks placed at a 45-degree angle with the line of circulation. Each is three stories high creating nine units, each an open central office space with partitioned offices along two sides of the square. Other areas—a boardroom, a lecture hall, a conference area, and lounge—are separate units also connected to the spine.

Each of the nine office units is, in a sense, a self-contained identity with its own reception point, private offices, secretarial areas, partially enclosed work stations and open "pool" area organized in much the fashion of more conventional office planning. Each unit includes a corner conference room as well. The scale of the units makes it possible to place all private spaces on a window wall while still making the opposite window wall available to the open pool area. This way the entire staff has access to outside light and view.

Photograph by Nick Wheeler, plan and photograph courtesy ISD, Inc.

A Stanford campus gymnasium built in 1921 had become obsolete for its original uses. The space was filled with temporary offices, when events made it reasonable to ask if the facility could be made permanently useful. With 17,000 sq. ft. of floor space and a vast, 48-foot ceiling height, an open plan approach seemed the only possible way of making something useful out of such cavernous space. Herman Miller's "Action Office" system was chosen as the primary tool for making workable work stations that could comfortably accommodate approximately 110 people and still preserve flexibility. Each staff person was interviewed to determine detailed equipment and communication needs.

Acoustical problems seemed threatening in such a vast, reverberant space. A six-inch raised floor (helpful with wiring problems) carpeted on top, and "tents" of canvas over typing and EDP areas where noise production was at a maximum, dealt with these problems. There is an elevated platform defining a reception and exhibit area, and a balcony along one wall provides space for private conference areas. The results are visually spectacular, while user acceptance has been outstanding. The combination of an individually accommodating furniture system with the grand scale of the total open space seems to be particularly acceptable.

Stanford University

PERSONNEL AND ARCHITECTURAL PLANNING DEPARTMENTS

Stanford, California
**Barry Brukoff, office planner
and interior designer**

Open "Action Office" work stations create human-scaled spaces within the cavernous former gymnasium. A carpeted, raised floor helps minimize acoustic problems.

Photographs courtesy Barry Brukoff and Herman Miller, Inc.

Each staff member was interviewed to determine his or her individual needs. This typical work station has a conference table in the foreground, locked and open storage areas, and greenery.

An elevated platform defines the reception and exhibit area. The overhead lighting adds to the aesthetic as well as practical interest of the office.

Willis, Faber and Dumas
Ipswich, England
Norman Foster, Associates, architects

This three-story plus penthouse, glass-sheathed building houses some twelve hundred work stations. The main entrance lobby opens up in a well where twin escalators travel up through the two working floors and into the skylit penthouse. Behind the lobby on the ground floor, a glass wall gives a view of the 75-foot swimming pool. The central well ties the interior levels together in a way that gives the whole building a sense of openness and unity. The office floors, interrupted only by service blocks, extend outward to the glass perimeter wall which wraps around the irregularly curved building form set by the site. Circulation space along this glass perimeter gives all the building's occupants easy access to the visual openness that the floor-to-ceiling glass provides.

At roof level, the escalators terminate in a rectangular penthouse given over to a restaurant, also glass-walled, that looks out over a roof garden which amounts to almost an acre of open space. The ground floor includes a gymnasium, a nursery, and a bar! Office work areas are totally open in the manner of original Bürolandschaft projects. The visually dramatic escalator links the special amenities into a close-knit unit with actual work space. The all-glass exterior makes the building externally spectacular— a mirrorlike reflective mass by day; an open, lighted pavilion at night. A special "armored" solar control glazing makes the building acceptably energy efficient. The integrated ceiling incorporates lighting, acoustical control, HVAC distribution, and a sprinkler system—a significant factor in making the entire building acceptable for fire-safety.

Photographs by Ken Kirkwood, courtesy Norman Foster Associates

Twin escalators (above) travel up through the building, linking the working floors (above right) and the skylit, penthouse level (right), which offers a view of the work levels below.

The spectacular, curving glass, walled exterior is transparent by night but mirrorlike by day. The office floors extend outward to the glass perimeter wall.

Technical Issues

Every office project, whatever its aesthetic and visible characteristics, is also an exercise in dealing with a range of technical problems. How well technical problems are solved has an impact on the level of user satisfaction, but also has an economic impact that cannot be ignored. The goal, it would seem, is to marshall technical issues in a way that generates a maximum of user satisfaction and effectiveness along with minimal cost. It is a matter of cost/benefit ratio, but with the costs sometimes hard to pin down and with the benefits even less subject to specific evaluation.

While it may not seem a specifically *technical* issue, all other issues must refer back to the space assigned to each office worker. Open planning is sometimes supported on the basis of its ability to cut back on space requirements by squeezing more people into less space. Savings in circulation spaces, shared in open planning, are the main source of such predicted gains. In practice, using open planning to economize on rental space has a history of being unwise. Open plan work stations are most likely to serve well when they are generous, not stingy. Possibilities for absorption of added work stations or future expansion are defeated when space assignments are pared to a minimum. Every situation must develop its own set of space standards, but some rough guidelines can be suggested on the basis of current practical experience. A typical space standard might be:

Senior executive	250–450 sq. ft.
Executive	200–350 sq. ft.
Middle manager	100–250 sq. ft.
Supervisor	100–150 sq. ft.
Professional	100–200 sq. ft.
Clerical staff	50–100 sq. ft.

To the above, must be added an allowance for general circulation of ten to twenty percent and specific allowance for

Exposed ducts, ambient lighting, and task lighting here illustrate an unusual approach to technical considerations. Aesthetics and practicality are well matched in this older loft building. (Offices of ISD, Inc. in Chicago, Illinois)

functions such as reception and waiting areas, conference and meeting spaces, filing and storage, rest and food-service areas, and any other ancillary functions of the particular project.

The service function most closely related to area assignment is HVAC (heating, ventilation, and air-conditioning). Dramatic cost increases for these services has made studying the implications of design proposals on HVAC costs standard practice in new buildings. Older buildings were often planned with little thought to energy consumption and its implications. When considering rental space, costs may be "buried" in the rent, but the direct environmental impacts cannot be dismissed so easily. Window walls are particularly problematic. In warm weather, west-facing glass surfaces can generate heat build-up, particularly late in the day, that available air-conditioning cannot cope with. Any large glass areas can cause a heat-loss problem in winter, leading to makeshift efforts to offset chill using highly uneconomic portable heaters. Many new products—such as thermal blinds and heat-shield glazing materials—are available to help in dealing with such problems, but no really satisfactory substitute exists for energy awareness in basic building design.

Lighting is closely tied into energy issues. Footcandle standards can be converted to wattage demand for any given lighting design, and wattage converts to an energy bill which represents both the cost of providing the lighting and the secondary cost of removing with extra air-conditioning the heat generated by the energy consumption of lighting equipment.

Levels of illumination, measured in footcandles, are the easiest characteristics of lighting installations to measure; a simple light meter gives a direct reading. For many years, meeting published standards for footcandle levels was regarded as a sufficient test of lighting adequacy. Suggested levels were constantly increased on the basis of questionable research that suggested that more lighting was always better. Rising energy costs have forced a reexamination of this viewpoint. The light of a candle one foot away will measure to be about one footcandle. Outdoor daylight in sun will reach six thousand to eight thousand footcandles. The human eye adjusts automatically (like the iris of a modern camera) throughout most of this range. For office work, one candle would seem inadequate and bright sun a bit much, but between about twenty and two thousand footcandles, most tasks will seem satisfactorily lighted *if* certain other standards are met as well. For the sake of economy, low intensity levels are preferable but, to take care of demanding seeing tasks (fine print, columns of figures) and of the needs of people with eye problems, levels well above the minimum are usually recommended. A table of modern standards suggests:

	footcandles
Passages and storage areas	5
Stairways and shipping areas	10
Ambient light in offices	10
Reading and writing (minimum)	20
Reading fine print	25
Typing and bookkeeping	30
Prolonged "close work"	50
Drafting	50–70

Unfortunately, efforts to meet such standards often lead to unsatisfactory lighting through neglect of other problems. If both bright and dim areas exist within the field of vision, the eye has trouble adjusting to both levels. "Excessive brightness contrast," too wide a spread between bright and dim, makes it difficult to see well even where the footcandle level at the main task is satisfactory. Bright fixtures visible in the ceiling or a bright window at a distance can create excessive contrast by injecting too bright a point; a dark desk top or floor can create a similar problem by surrounding a bright main task with a dim background. Suggested ratios of brightest to dimmest points in the field of view are:

Task to immediate background	5:1 maximum
Task to general surrounding area	20:1 maximum
Light source to surrounding enclosure	40:1 maximum
Maximum anywhere in the field	80:1 maximum

While these spreads may seem quite large, a glaring light fixture can easily create a far larger ratio than the maximum considered acceptable. Light sources must be shielded from direct view to keep brightness contrast within acceptable limits while desk tops and work surfaces should be a light color. Ceiling light fixtures are a particular source of trouble; only those with "low-brightness" louvers or lenses should be considered despite their higher cost and slightly lower efficiency as compared to simple fixtures with bare tubes or a glaring diffusing lens.

Another problem arises when the light source is positioned so that the task surface reflects glare into the user's eyes. If a mirror placed on the task surface reflects an image of the source, this is evidence that an objectionable situation exists. Even though the surface (paper, print, keyboard) is not a reflector, there will be enough reflectivity to cause "veiling reflections," a haze of light that makes vision more difficult, particularly when the surface is somewhat glossy. Everyone has experienced moving a glossy magazine page or photograph about to avoid this annoyance. Ceiling lights and lights placed close to desk-top level in front of the user are likely to create this problem. The solution is a combination of relocating the light source to angle reflection right or left. Lenses or louvers that angle the flux of light so as to block veiling reflections are a possible alternative. A standard called ESI (for equivalent sphere illumination, a description of the testing method used) has been developed to create a one-number standard to express the effectiveness of lighting in terms of ease of seeing (taking into account both level of illumination and effects of reflection). Expressed in footcandles, it gives a better idea of the merit of a lighting installation than the "raw" footcandles as indicated by a simple meter. A table of suggested ESI illumination standards is similar to the earlier "raw" footcandle tables. For example:

	ESI footcandles
Passage and storage areas	5–10
Stairways and shipping areas	5–20
Ambient light in offices	10–30
Reading and writing	30–70
Reading fine print, typing, bookkeeping	50–100
Prolonged close work and drafting	100–200

Energy economy has led away from the earlier practice of lighting an entire office space with a high footcandle level at desk top. This means overlighting a large portion of the office space. By moving the light source close to the task at hand, much less light can provide for excellent vision. The term "task lighting" refers to this close-up provision of light sources, generally as an integral part of an office system. To prevent circulation and other spaces from being too dim, ambient light is provided in several ways—by directing a portion of the task lighting upward to the ceiling; by providing additional, separate ambient light fixtures or "kiosks," or by including ceiling fixtures with low-brightness lenses, or louvers, spaced to provide only ambient "fill" lighting. Combinations of these techniques are also possible.

Economy of a lighting installation, (considering power consumption and the resulting air-conditioning loads) can be evaluated in terms of watts per square foot provided. A measure of 2.5 watts per sq. ft. is reasonable, but 1.5 watts per sq. ft. is attainable in truly efficient installations. Older installations often consume 5 to 10 watts per sq. ft. The modern open office is often heavily equipped with VDT units that pose a special problem. Their screens are glossy and reflective while the figures and letters they display are small, sometimes dim, sometimes bright, and seemingly flickering. VDT screens need to be shaded from direct reflections; users should be able to tilt and adjust them, back to front, to suit their needs. Eye and other physical problems can develop in workers who constantly use VDTs where proper care has not been taken to adjust lighting and positioning.

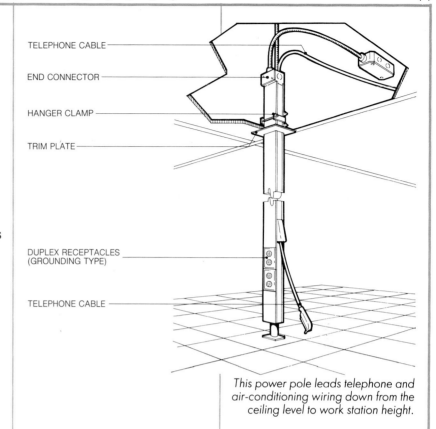

TELEPHONE CABLE

END CONNECTOR

HANGER CLAMP

TRIM PLATE

DUPLEX RECEPTACLES (GROUNDING TYPE)

TELEPHONE CABLE

This power pole leads telephone and air-conditioning wiring down from the ceiling level to work station height.

Wiring presents another set of technical problems. Almost every workplace now requires connections for a telephone, a typewriter, and other electrical equipment (including the proliferating VDTs). In addition, VDTs require special communications cabling while computer equipment often requires a separate ("dedicated") power supply. Some printers, copy machines, and other devices have further special requirements for power and other wiring. Task lighting is another power consumer at desk level. Leading this net of wiring into open office space, bringing it to the individual wired devices at their respective workplaces, and doing this with reasonable neatness is a particularly troublesome problem of modern office design. When it is also noted that frequent changes in wiring are to be anticipated, the problem becomes even more difficult.

Older office buildings usually provide under-floor ducts for wires leading to floor outlets mounted where removable capping plates are located. Such systems are often not adequate for modern needs and are usually relatively inflexible. For offices with a heavy concentration of power and communications wiring, for computer rooms, brokerage and trading room installations, the best modern solution is a raised or "access" floor. This is a floor of lift-out panels supported

above the building floor on stilts or posts, usually at a height between six and eighteen inches above the original floor. The under-floor space becomes an open "plenum" where wires and cables can be run freely and within which changes can be made easily.

Unfortunately, an access floor is expensive, requires enough ceiling height to accept the loss of height dimension, and poses the problem of steps or ramps where the raised area begins and ends. For offices with less intensive wiring requirements, under-floor ducts are still often used, wiring in the ceiling may be considered (with its requirement for "poles" or other means of dropping wires to work stations), or the newer "flat wiring" that can be taped down to a floor and covered over with carpet squares may serve. In all cases, the wiring provisions of modern office systems must lead wiring from an access point to the individual work station and precise location of the wired equipment.

Acoustical problems are a particular issue in open offices. Without solid walls, noise is not confined, conversations in near locations may become distracting, and there is often a sense of privacy loss. Indeed, this is the aspect of open planning most often mentioned in opposing its acceptance for new projects and in criticizing existing installations. With proper planning, acoustical problems can be dealt with, but some care must be taken to avoid a distressing situation when the new office is first occupied. Problems can be dealt with after they surface, but it may be difficult to counteract bad first impressions.

The first acoustical issue is noise. Many people at work can generate a noise level high enough to be an annoyance. It is now generally accepted that an open office must have carpeted floors and a ceiling with good sound absorption qualities. Perimeter walls and partitions with sound-reflective surfaces also need acoustical treatment to make them as absorptive as possible. Glass perimeter walls are a particular problem. Screen panels, file surrounds, and other vertical elements of systems furniture can contribute to noise control with sound-absorptive surfaces. A combination of these steps usually drops sound levels well below annoyance level and may, in fact, produce an environment that is too quiet (as discussed below). An exception arises where noisy machines are in use. Typewriters, long a major problem, are now giving way to quieter word processing equipment. Printers associated with computer installations are, however, often extremely noisy. Special housings can control noise from typewriters, and other loud devices. Their use is almost mandatory unless the noisy machines can be isolated in closed rooms.

Having achieved a quiet open office, another problem

occurs. Near conversation becomes all too audible in the otherwise silent space. It is important that individual workspaces be placed as far apart as possible and oriented to avoid a direct forward path for sound travel. Next, screen panels should minimize transmission of sound. This is a matter often overemphasized in manufacturers' literature, where test results suggest that screens form effective sound barriers. Since these panels do not extend to the ceiling and are not sealed at the edges and floor, screens can do no more than slightly retard sound transmission. Their acoustical characteristics can help to some degree, but this is a minor factor in dealing with the problems of overheard speech.

The most effective control in the open space is the presence of random, ambient noise, a background hum not loud enough to be an annoyance but strong enough to make speech at a nearby work station unintelligible. This is a familiar effect in restaurants, where no privacy exists but where conversations at neighboring tables are not annoying because they blend into random background sound. Restaurants are, in fact, favorite places for private and confidential talk. In the open office, the ideal background hum has a level of around 50 to 60 decibels in the frequencies of normal speech. With proper treatment, such levels will be developed naturally, but since user activity may vary (a quiet time may occur at lunch hour when many people are absent or in an unused conference area), it is generally necessary to provide an artificial source of background noise. A sound system of many small speakers in concealed ceiling locations and a central sound generator produce "white" or "gray" noise, a mixture of frequencies that mask speech without being particularly noticeable in themselves. An ideal masking sound system is not "heard" by office users but completes the task of making the acoustical environment satisfactory.

Remaining technical issues relate to matters of safety and security. Office fires, particularly in high buildings, have become a matter of increasing concern. Some fire codes require large open office spaces to be subdivided with fire-rated walls to limit fire spread—a detriment to open office planning concepts. Modern materials, particularly synthetics used in carpet, upholstery, and window treatments, pose fire risks because of the production of toxic fumes when burning. Dense power wiring presents its own fire risks. Proper emergency exit provisions are vital, especially since the most effective fire protection systems—ceiling sprinklers—remain unpopular because of their significant initial cost.

Security against intrusion, theft, vandalism, and even industrial spying may present problems for some organizations. In many cases, intelligent layout can do a great deal to minimize such worries. The open plan, although it makes locked rooms rare, substitutes ease of direct visual observation that acts as a deterrent to many forms of trouble. Office furniture systems usually provide locks for components, making locked rooms unnecessary. Room locks are not very effective, in any case, since rooms can rarely be kept locked because of the practical needs of access for cleaning and maintenance. Electronic techniques are also available to deal with more difficult problems. Card or combination number locks, closed-circuit television surveillance systems, and a wide range of detection and alarm systems are available which, combined with intelligent planning, can minimize problems that have become acute in older buildings in central city areas.

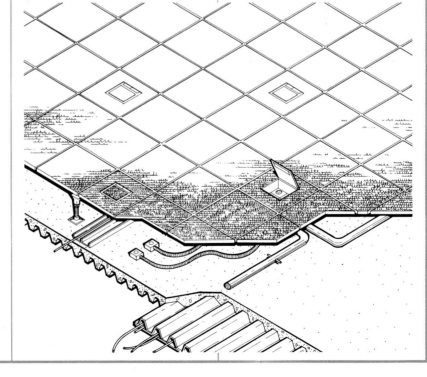

In this cut-away view of access flooring, wiring "pockets" are shown both open and closed. The actual wiring systems lead from these pockets out to the appropriate electrical or other source. The photographs on the facing page define the wiring pockets more clearly.

The Office of the Future

For some years magazine articles, conferences, and planning groups have been obsessed with discussions of "the office of the future" or, as it was often called, the coming "electronic office." As seems to happen so often, by the time various authorities manage to predict what lies ahead, reality outstrips the predictions. Modern offices became electronic before anyone had time to grasp what that meant. It is a cliché to say that the office of the future has already arrived.

The existing future-oriented office includes computer use as a normal office function. A CRT unit (VDT and keyboard) appears at a large percentage of work stations, in many fields moving toward 90 to 100 percent. Paper—handwritten, typed, and carbon-copied—has given way to electronic communication, viewed on a screen, filed on magnetic media or in micrographic form and printed, when needed, by one of a number of efficient printers. Keyboards are everywhere, fixed and portable and able to transmit keyed-in material over phone lines to and from remote locations throughout the world. Conferences can take place between remote participants with spoken, and sometimes visual, contact. Written materials can be read automatically, funds transferred electronically. Banking and brokerage routines have been automated to a point unthinkable even ten years ago. If the office of the future has arrived with such speed and force, the issue of "What next?" becomes all the more pressing. No one expects change and progress to stop here and now—but what is next?

A number of predictions are about and one can suppose that, like most future predictions, they include a mix of what will indeed happen, perhaps more quickly than expected, together with a certain fallout of events that now seem likely to occur but that will never materialize.

Although built in 1972, the offices of Centraal Beheer are "futuristic" in concept—the architect's concern with the building as a humane workplace led to a decision to forego vast open floors and substitute clusters of small modules.

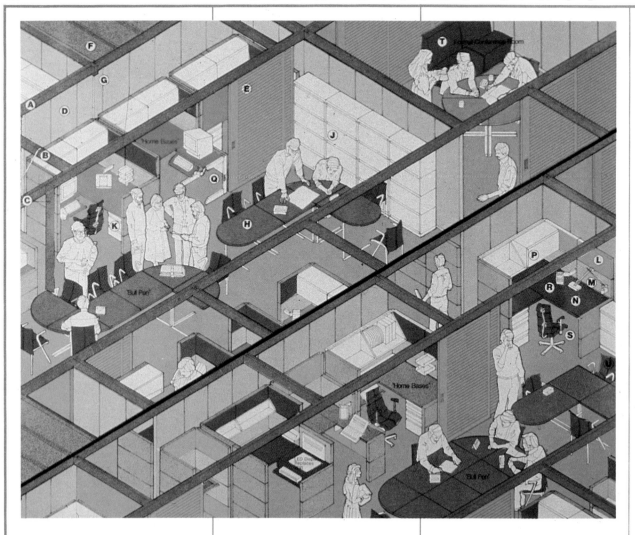

A "behavior settings approach" to office design as proposed in a competition entry by Robert Luchetti and Philip Stone. Work stations are multipurpose and can be opened up or divided as required.

in suburban locations convenient to nothing except, perhaps, the homes of a few top executives? The costs of real estate and the costs of commuting, the latter in both time and money, are staggering. Home computers are already creating a class of independent office workers who hardly need to leave their bedrooms to carry on successful careers as financial traders, researchers, or writers. If one imagines the home terminal upgraded to include full television visual imaging, to permit remote conversations and conferences, it becomes possible to predict a totally dispersed office with workers coming to a "head office" only for occasional training and discussions, much as field salespeople now attend an annual sales meeting to reestablish personal connections to their company. If the remote office terminal can be portable as well, the dispersed office can be imagined as totally fluid. Objections to the costs of the complex communications nets involved must be evaluated in relation to the staggering costs of residence in congested megalopolis areas and the costs of commuting on

failing public transit or in wasteful private cars.

Along with such predictions, one must consider the probability that office work will itself become more fully automated. It is already possible to do most banking transactions at an automated terminal. Travel and car rental arrangements are made electronically at a computerized central memory unit that is in some remote location to most of its users. As the public develops familiarity with VDT communication, and as the VDT is replaced by simpler communication units, many businesses can look forward to near total automation of office work. OCR units can read incoming orders and produce shipping orders and billing as well as internal reporting, all without human intervention. The automatic office connected to an automatic factory suggests industry operating with minimal personnel. Many government services (tax collection, social security, drivers' licenses) operate in much this way already with live workers involved only, at the low end, in dealing directly with citizens not yet

Plan courtesy Robert Luchetti and Philip Stone

fully "on-line" and, at the high end, in dealing with problem situations and planning new strategies and actions. A brokerage house or an insurance company could, even now, take a step toward full automation.

The change hinted at here is roughly parallel to the change in telephone offices from the old "central" with rows of operators at switchboards, to the modern office which is simply a hive of automatic gear watched over by a few maintenance people. As equipment shrinks, one can expect the central office of a large organization to be no more than a box of automatic equipment in touch with a dispersed office staff (at home or at some spa perhaps) and with its public by strictly electronic means. The need for some direct contact for problem solving, planning, and what are usually thought of as the top managerial tasks of "decision-making" will still exist, although some of these functions could also be dispersed. The residue would probably survive at a headquarters, but that would hardly need to be the ostentatious plant that is now standard.

In fact, top meetings and decision-making might well be shifted to restaurants, hotels, or other nonoffice locations. International summit conferences, meetings of top executives, and corporate sales meetings are already usually conducted away from any regular office setting. Why should this not become a more universal practice?

Such predictions suggest, of course, vast reductions in needs for office staff. Combined with the reductions in work force in industry and agriculture, specters of increasing unemployment, with related social and political implications, arise. Reduction in the need for human work (defined as necessary, gainful work as distinguished from strictly voluntary activities) must be viewed as a net gain for humanity, although an increasing effort to face problems of distributing work (and the income generated) equitably to diminish a major unemployment problem will be necessary. The average work day may well shrink to a few hours or minutes at a portable communications device. Free time will become increasingly available for private life, for voluntary activities, and for inventive and creative activities that can lead to further human benefits.

Reality suggests that change will come rapidly in some places, slowly in others. While some offices may virtually vanish into electronic communication, others will surely remain in various mixes of conventional, open, and electronic forms while still others may cling to rolltop desks, massive account books with steel pen entries, and green eyeshades. In the modern world of spacecraft, submarines, and television, we still have bicycles, rowboats, and oil paintings. Offices will, no doubt, continue with a similar mix.

Predictions begin with a consideration of changes that can be expected in the detailed nature of office equipment. Computers have already become small, but it is quite certain that they will become even smaller and less expensive. A large computer will probably be available in matchbox size while a giant "mainframe" can be expected to diminish to a desk-size box within another ten to twenty years. The bulk of most computers will be determined by their input and output devices. The latter, now generally the bulky CRT, can be expected to become a "flat screen," a panel of negligible thickness. Keyboard size is already fairly minimal, but "flat" versions can be expected along with flat "slates" for written or drawn input. Reduced power requirements should help reduce the present tangles of wiring. Phone and other communications cabling may gradually give way to less troublesome media. Fiber-optics can make cables nonelectrical. Radio, infrared, light and laser beam communication are all in the offing, promising freedom from wires. Devices can still be expected to require power, but low-current demand could permit battery power to take over and eliminate AC power wiring for many devices. Lighting remains a problem as long as task lighting continues to represent the current best solution. Light beamed overhead from central laser sources and then redirected and diffused to illuminate individual work stations has been proposed as an escape from power wiring needs.

Small equipment and minimal wiring needs would tend to bring real mobility to work stations. This leads to suggestions for wheeled work stations, which would allow groupings to change from day to day or even on a moment's notice. Also, it is not such a long leap to imagine a work station that could be either open or partially or totally closed to accommodate the user's need for privacy and isolation. Putting these ideas together gives rise to a rather surprising sort of office, something like a parking garage filled with mobile units with convertible tops up or down as occupants require. A "core" of fixed elements might include conference rooms, storage areas, and other necessities for common use. Such proposals still assume the need for an office location where a staff assembles daily to be in close personal touch.

Another proposal often discussed suggests that the need for an assembled staff is far less than commonly supposed. With instant electronic communication, any worker with access to screen and keyboard is able to carry on most office work activities anywhere at all—at home, at a vacation spot, even in an airplane. Why then build vast office buildings located in crowded city centers that suit the supposed need for proximity to other offices, services, and workers' homes or, alternatively,

Impact and Evaluation

The basic question about open office planning is, naturally enough, does it work? How well does it work? What are its benefits measured in specific and understandable terms? Such questions have been in the air since the first landscape office plans appeared. Opponents of the idea asserted that open offices simply would not, did not, "work." A number of articles and conference remarks stated that the open plan was a fad, an unworkable proposal that would quickly disappear as its shortcomings were discovered.

Early open offices went into service in Europe in 1964. Most of these are still in regular use. Now, about 50 percent of new office space is planned in open fashion. Any thought that the whole idea is a momentary aberration destined to be forgotten within months is obviously not related to reality—open planning is taking over office design. Certainly, conventional offices still exist, and many projects now mix conventional and open planning. However, the makers of office furniture are turning more and more toward the systems that imply open plan. According to BIFMA, the Business and Institutional Furniture Manufacturers' Association, a compiler of data on the basis of annual surveys, more than 50 percent of office furniture in current production is aimed at open plan situations. This certainly indicates that the open office is much more than a fad.

This still leaves the question of effectiveness open to discussion. Wide adoption of a particular approach is not, in itself, proof that the approach is sound. Validation of the success of open planning is still often hard to locate.

What is success? Is it a matter of user satisfaction? User satisfaction is fairly easy to test but it raises more questions than it settles. In general, any number of test situations have shown that office staff moved into a new, open plan installation will report significant favorable reactions. The new installation is, after all, being judged in comparison with an older situation that had probably become obsolescent. People who had occupied bullpen space will generally find the work stations of an open plan project a distinct improvement. Negatives come, most often, from middle-management levels where hopes for a status-oriented private space have been thwarted by the open office predilection for no walls.

The middle level usually grumbles about loss of privacy, but with its identification with managerial goals, will usually support the larger aims of open planning in terms of work efficiency and flexibility. The hard questions must evaluate whether open offices genuinely produce gains in office work productivity. This is difficult territory to probe with any clarity. What is office productivity? Is it a matter of the numbers of letters typed, orders processed, or similar measurable tasks? Such matters can be measured, but since the new office usually introduces new equipment and new work processes along with new layout, there is rarely a clear test case available to show gains based on planning practice alone. Even clear gains may be challenged on the basis of the "Hawthorne effect," that well-known phenomenon which brings about measurable improvement as the result of the very fact that testing is in progress. Besides, office work is no longer primarily a matter of output of standard forms or letters. Such work is becoming increasingly automated.

Productivity in an office is a matter of good decisions efficiently developed—high morale leading to quality performance and a decline in absenteeism, employee turnover, and similar evidences of office malaise. How can one measure the effectiveness of the open office in such areas, separating the impact of the office facility from such other influences as management style, and policies about pay and promotion? The available studies do not do too well. Many are sponsored by furniture manufacturers with an obvious interest in supporting a particular point of view—a situation tainting the validity of test findings. Others come from organization managements with a similar desire to prove that what has been done was for the best. Most surveys and studies are "opinion surveys," that is, studies of what people *think* is better or worse not studies that can measure actualities independent of opinion.

Still, findings take on a certain weight in the aggregate, however uncertain the research techniques may seem. Note first the paucity, indeed, total absence, of any reports fundamentally negative to open planning success. Perhaps the most negative validated report to be found, itself merely noncommittal, came from the early DuPont Corporation test of a doctrinaire landscape office floor in direct comparison with a conventionally planned floor in the same building for a comparable corporate division. The finding was no clear finding. The two spaces seemed about equal when opinions, pro and con, were balanced out. This can be interpreted as a finding in favor of the open plan, of course, if one postulates the almost undeniable gains of the open approach in terms of flexibility for future readjustments.

Other negative reports flow most often by word of mouth and seem to refer to intances in which open planning was badly planned or executed. A major furniture company, for example, ironically the maker of a well-regarded office system, installed its own offices without any consideration for acoustical problems (a hard plaster ceiling insured problems of noise and inadequate privacy). Loud complaints from users followed, but these must be attributed to the failure of project planning rather than to the system concept.

A recent study by BOSTI (Buffalo Organization for Social and Technological Innovation) under the direction of Michael Brill, suggests that real improvements can be validated in recent open offices, even though the survey technique is still opinion rather than a form of statistical measurement. BOSTI surveyed new offices, predominantly open in plan concept, and found a wide consensus among workers and managers that improved office environmental conditions did improve both quantity and quality of work production. Specific statistics support the observation that absenteeism and turnover drop with improved work settings. The specific findings with special impact on open planning are those that show that a sense of privacy at the workplace is important and that workers generally do not feel any significant sense of privacy unless enclosure is present on three sides of the seated worker with panels or partitions extending above head height. This finding is clearly negative to totally open, landscape concepts, and favorable to panel and furniture systems that offer the degree of enclosure suggested.

A further finding, less significant for planning concepts, but with impact on office design in visual terms, suggests that office staff is unenthusiastic about white, gray, and neutral color schemes with occasional sharp accent colors so often preferred by professional designers. Warm "homey" colors, textures, and materials such as natural woods are much preferred and are related to improved work performance. Designers are challenged by this finding to discover a way to adjust to such preferences without reverting to heavy and tasteless combinations of imitation woodgrains with harsh red and orange fabric colors—perhaps "homey" but hardly the elements that will make a suitable and acceptable office environment.

A search for reports that measure actual productivity in open plan offices in comparison with conventional offices produces too many comparisons in which the conventional office is an "old" office, in use for many years and, one may suppose, shabby, drab, and generally outmoded. *Any* new office, open or otherwise, could be expected to be an improvement so that findings in favor of the new office may be attributable to newness as much as to openness. This objection does not apply to findings that relate to costs of rearrangement, maintenance, etc., where specific dollar values can be related to one plan type as compared to the other.

A few typical reports are summarized here:

Since 1970, Eastman Kodak has rearranged over 1.5 million sq. ft. of open office space at an average cost of about $1 per sq. ft. Comparable reconfiguration of drywall partitioned space would range from $6 to $30 per sq. ft. This suggests a minimum saving of $5 per sq. ft. whenever replanning takes place. Other estimates suggest costs of rearranging open space may be as little as $.75 or even $.50.

Facility Management Institute provides estimates indicating that savings in operation and maintenance costs of 10 to 20 percent in HVAC costs are realized in open plan projects because a uniform, centralized system can serve a large, open area with maximum efficiency.

In the United States, tax benefits often accrue to users of open planning because screening, which is part of a furniture system, takes the place of fixed partition walls. Walls are classified as part of building structure and so are subject to a longer depreciation schedule. Screens, classified as furnishings, provide a 10 percent investment write-off.

Evaluation of an open office in Minneapolis for McQuay-Perfex, Inc. generated a saving resulting from improved productivity on the part of the 430 employees of about $200,000 in one year's time, without including any benefits from increased flexibility, tax benefits, or other such considerations.

A time and motion study at the Centralized Services Bureau of the Internal Revenue Service showed a saving of 7.4 percent of employee work time through elimination of waste movement in open work stations as compared to conventional desk set-ups.

At a Blue Cross/Blue Shield facility in Detroit a before-and-after study showed work output stabilized at 112.5 percent of the "before" record in the new, open office.

At two new Wells Fargo Bank installations (at Santa Ana and Walnut Creek, California) comparison of employee turnover showed a drop from 17.2 to 9.6 percent. It was also noted in this study that morale among middle-management executives was maintained despite changeover from private to open offices.

While none of these findings may seem totally conclusive about every aspect of open plan benefits, they build up an aggregate impression of *no* negative findings, the positive findings ranging from small to large in one or another area studied. Since the excellence of open installations is subject to considerable variation, it seems reasonable to assume that the best open projects are strikingly advantageous. Constant improvement in equipment design and in planning skills will make future open plan projects still better.

Useful Addresses

The following list is a resource guide to sources of information within the United States, Canada, the United Kingdom, and many other countries. Included are addresses for associations, office furniture sources, manufacturers and suppliers, building products, equipment, and magazines.

Office Furniture: United States and Canada

ALL-STEEL, INC.
P.O. Box 871, Route 31 and
Ashland Avenue
Aurora, Illinois 60507
Tel.: 312-859-2600

ALMA DESK COMPANY
P.O. Box 2250
High Point, North Carolina 27261
Tel.: 919-885-4101

AMERICAN DESK
P.O. Box 429 or
49 and West Avenue G
Temple, Texas 76501
Tel.: 817-773-1776

AMERICAN SEATING COMPANY
902 Broadway Avenue, N.W.
Grand Rapids, Michigan 49504
Tel.: 616-456-0600

ATELIER INTERNATIONAL LTD.
595 Madison Avenue
New York, New York 10022
Tel.: 212-644-0400

BRICKEL ASSOCIATES, INC.
515 Madison Avenue
New York, New York 10022
Tel.: 212-688-2233

C I DESIGNS
574 Boston Avenue
Medford, Massachusetts 02155
Tel.: 617-391-7800

CASTELLI FURNITURE, INC.
950 Third Avenue, 9th Floor
New York, New York 10022
Tel.: 212-751-2050

FACIT
66 Field Point Road
Greenwich, Connecticut 06830
Tel.: 203-622-9150

GF BUSINESS EQUIPMENT, INC.
229 East Dennick Avenue
Youngstown, Ohio 44501
Tel.: 216-746-7271

HALLER SYSTEMS, INC.
8687 Melrose Avenue Number 257
Los Angeles, California 90069
Tel.: 213-854-1109

HARDWOOD HOUSE, INC.
569 Lyell Avenue
Rochester, New York 14606
Tel.: 716-254-0600

HARTER CORPORATION
910 Prairie Avenue
Sturgis, Michigan 49091
Tel.: 616-651-3201

E.F. HAUSERMAN COMPANY
5711 Grant Avenue
Cleveland, Ohio 44105
Tel.: 216-883-1400; 800-321-8698

HAWORTH, INC.
One Haworth Center
Holland, Michigan 49423
Tel.: 616-392-5961; 800-632-3892

ICF, INC. (INTERNATIONAL
CONTRACT FURNISHERS)
305 East 63rd Street
New York, New York 10021
Tel.: 212-750-0900

JG FURNITURE SYSTEMS, A
DIVISION OF BURLINGTON
INDUSTRIES
121 Park Avenue
Quakertown, Pennsylvania 18951
Tel.: 215-536-7343

JSI (JASPER SEATING COMPANY)
932 Mill Street
Jasper, Indiana 47546
Tel.: 812-482-3204

KNOLL INTERNATIONAL
The Knoll Building
655 Madison Avenue
New York, New York 10021
Tel.: 212-826-2400; 800-223-1354

KREUGER
1330 Bellevue Street
P.O. Box 8100
Green Bay, Wisconsin 54308

LEHIGH-LEOPOLD FURNITURE
2825 Mount Pleasant Street
Burlington, Iowa 52601
Tel.: 319-753-2271; 800-553-2371

MILLER, HERMAN, INC.
8500 Byron Road
Zeeland, Michigan 49464
Tel.: 616-772-3300

PROBBER, HARVEY, INC.
44 Probber Lane
Fall River, Massachusetts 02726
Tel.: 617-674-3591

ROSE JOHNSON
1111 Godfrey Avenue, S.W.
Grand Rapids, Michigan 49503
Tel.: 616-245-2103

SHAW WALKER COMPANY
P.O. Box 209
Muskegon, Michigan 49443
Tel.: 616-722-7211

STEELCASE, INC.
1120 36th Street, S.E.
Grand Rapids, Michigan 49501
Tel.: 616-247-2710

STENDIG, INC.
410 East 62nd Street
New York, New York 10021
Tel.: 212-838-6050

STORWAL INTERNATIONAL,
INC.
901 Merchandise Mart
Number 901
Chicago, Illinois 60654
Tel.: 312-822-9240

STOW/DAVIS
25 Summer Avenue
Grand Rapids, Michigan 49504
Tel.: 616-456-9681

SUNAR, LTD.
18 Marshall Street
Norwalk, Connecticut 06854
Tel.: 203-866-3100

THONET INDUSTRIES
491 East Princess Street
P.O. Box 1587
York, Pennsylvania 17405
Tel.: 717-845-6666

VECTA CONTRACT, INC.
1800 South Great Southwest Parkway
Grand Prairie, Texas 75051
Tel.: 214-641-2860

WESTINGHOUSE ELECTRIC
CORPORATION,
ARCHITECTURAL SYSTEMS
DIVISION
4300 36th Street, S.E.
Grand Rapids, Michigan 49508
Tel.: 616-949-1050

XCEPTION DESIGN, LTD.
2875 Industrial Boulevard
Laval, Quebec,
Canada H7L 3V8
Tel.: 514-668-0710

ZOGRAPHOS DESIGNS, LTD.
150 East 58th Street
New York, New York 10022
Tel.: 212-421-6650

FURNITURE FAIRS
Large trade fairs, in addition to exhibiting furniture, usually have a series of conferences, some of which address office design.

NEOCON is held annually in the Merchandise Mart in Chicago in June; IBS Birmingham (biennially October); SICOB Paris (September); Cologne Furniture Fair (biennially for office furniture); Milan (September).

Office Furniture: United Kingdom

FACIT OFFICE FURNITURE
DIVISION
3-4 Little Portland Street
London W1N 5AG
Tel.: 636-1164

HAUSERMAN, LTD.
Allen House
1 Westmead Road
Sutton, Surrey SM1 4JA
Tel.: 01-643-0835

HEAL CONTRACTS, LTD.
196 Tottenham Court Road
London W1A 1BJ
Tel.: 637-5232

HILLE INTERNATIONAL, LTD.
132 St. Albans Road
Watford, Hertfordshire WD2 4AG
Tel.: 92-42241

INTEGRATED FURNITURE
SYSTEMS, LTD.
44 Cathedral Place
London EC4M 7NQ
Tel.: 248-0712

LUCAS FURNITURE SYSTEMS
616 Wick Lane
London E3 2JJ
Tel.: 980-3232

HERMAN MILLER
149 Tottenham Court Road
London W1P 0JA

RACE FURNITURE
New Road
Sheerness, Kent
Tel.: 07956-2311

STEELCASE STRAFOR (UK),
LTD.
50-54 Southampton Row
London WC1B 4AR
Tel.: 405-4474/8

VOKO (UK), LTD.
11-14 Grafton Street
London W1X 3LA
Tel.: 629-5383

Office Furniture: West Germany

COMFORTO
Bergstrasse 1
D-4730 Ahlen
Tel.: 023-82/6631

GEBR. LÜBKE GmbH AND
COMPANY KG
Postfach 1660/3811
4840 Rheda-Wiedenbrück

KNOLL INTERNATIONAL
Simmenstrasse 1
7141 Murr/Murr

VOKO
Postfach 6540
63 Gieben 1

Office Furniture: Italy

ARFLEX
20051 Limbiate (Milan)
Via Monte Rosa 27
Tel.: 02-9961241

U.S.A. under license:
Beyleriam, Ltd.
305 East 63rd Street
New York, New York

ARTEMIDE
Via Brughiera
20010 Pregnan Milanese
Milan
Tel.: 02-9391255

CASSINA SpA
20036 Meda (Milan)
Via L Busnelli 1
Tel.: 0362-70581

CASTELLI
Bologna 40128
Via Torreggiani 1

KNOLL INTERNATIONAL
Via Flaminia 147
06034 Foligno (Perugia)

MARCATRE SpA
20020 Misinto (Milan)
Via Sant'Andrea 3
Tel.: 02-9648451

OLIVETTI SYNTHESIS
54100 Massa
Via Aurelia Ovest 65
Tel.: 0585-47811

TECNO
Via Bigle 22
Milan 20121
Tel.: 02-790341-4

Office Furniture: Sweden

FACIT
Luxbacken 1
L.Essingen
S 105 45 Stockholm
Tel.: 8-738-6000

Office Furniture: Finland

ARTEK
Keskuskatu 3
00100 Helsinki 10
Tel.: 90-177533

Office Furniture: Denmark

CADO THE ROYAL SYSTEM A/S
H. C. Andersens Boulevard 6
1553 Copenhagen V
Tel.: 01045-1111122

FRITZ HANSEN EFT A-S
DK-3450 Allerød
Tel.: 03-27-2300

Office Furniture: Switzerland

KNOLL INTERNATIONAL AG
Bernerstrasse Nord 208
CH-8064 Zurich

Office Furniture: France

AIRBORNE
3 Rue de Grenelle
75006 Paris
Tel.: 222-23-50

ARFLEX FRANCE SA
162 Boulevard Voltaire
Paris XI

ARTIFORT FRANCE
221 Rue Benoit Franchon
78500 Sartrouville
Tel.: 915-17-72

CASTELLI SA
13 Boulevard Ney
75018 Paris
Tel.: 200-32-00

FACIT DM
308 Rue du Président S Allende
92700 Colombes
Tel.: 780-71-17

KNOLL INTERNATIONAL
FRANCE
268 Boulevard St.-Germain
75007 Paris

LITTON MOBILIER DE BUREAU
7 Rue Mariotte
75017 Paris
Tel.: 261-80-00

Manufacturers and Suppliers: United States

ARCHITECTURAL
SUPPLEMENTS, INC.
150 East 58th Street
New York, New York 10022
Tel.: 212-758-0926
(Lighting and accessories)

ARTEMIDE, INC.
150 East 58th Street
New York, New York 10155
Tel.: 212-980-0710
(Lighting)

BEYLERIAN, LTD.
11 East 26th Street
New York, New York 10010
Tel.: 212-684-6650
(Accessories)

HABITAT, INC.
150 East 58th Street
New York, New York 10022
Tel.: 203-792-7400
(Lighting)

HALO LIGHTING, DIVISION
MCGRAW-EDISON COMPANY
400 Busse Road
Elk Grove, Illinois 60007
Tel.: 312-956-8400
(Lighting)

LIGHTING ASSOCIATES, INC.
305 East 63rd Street
New York, New York 10021
Tel.: 212-751-0575
(Lighting)

LIGHTOLIER, INC.
346 Claremont Avenue
Jersey City, New Jersey 07305
Tel.: 201-333-5120
(Lighting)

LUXO LAMP CORPORATION
Monument Park
Port Chester, New York 10573
Tel.: 914-937-4433
(Desk lamps)

NESSEN LAMPS, INC.
3200 Jerome Avenue
Bronx, New York 10468
Tel.: 212-295-0220
(Lighting)

PETER PEPPER PRODUCTS,
INC.
17929 South Susana Road
Compton, California 90221
Tel.: 213-979-0815
(Accessories)

SMITH METAL ARTS COMPANY,
INC.
1721 Elmwood Avenue
Buffalo, New York 14207
(Accessories)

Building Products: United States and Canada

ALCAN ALUMINUM
CORPORATION
100 Erieview Place
Cleveland, Ohio 44114
Tel.: 216-523-6800
(Ceilings)

ARMSTRONG WORLD
INDUSTRIES, INC.
P.O. Box 3001
Lancaster, Pennsylvania 17601
Tel.: 717-397-0611
(Ceilings and flooring)

BRAND-REX
Telecommunications Division
P.O. Box 498
Willimantic, Connecticut 06226
Tel.: 203-423-7783
(Undercarpet telephone cable)

COLLINS AND AIKMAN
CORPORATION COMMERCIAL
FLOOR SYSTEMS
210 Madison Avenue
New York, New York 10016
Tel.: 212-578-1217
(Carpeting)

DESIGN TEX FABRICS, INC.
56-08 37th Avenue
Woodside, New York 11377
Tel.: 212-335-9000
(Fabrics)

EDWARD FIELDS, INC.
232 East 59th Street, 2nd Floor
New York, New York 10022
Tel.: 212-759-2200
(Carpeting)

FORMS AND SURFACES
P.O. Box 5215
Santa Barbara, California 93108
Tel.: 805-969-4767
(Hardware)

GENERAL TIRE AND RUBBER
COMPANY/GTR
WALLCOVERING COMPANY
401 Hackensack Avenue, Suite 704
Hackensack, New Jersey 07601
Tel.: 201-489-0100
(Wallcovering)

GRANT HARDWARE COMPANY,
A DIVISION OF GRANT
INDUSTRIES, INC.
33A High Street
West Nyack, New York 10994-9967
Tel.: 914-358-4400
(Window covering)

HUNTER DOUGLAS, INC.
ARCHITECTURAL BUILDING
PRODUCTS DIVISION
P.O. Box 650
Durham, North Carolina 27702
Tel.: 800-334-8569
(Window coverings)

INTEGRATED CEILINGS, INC.
2231 Colby Avenue
Los Angeles, California 90064
Tel.: 213-272-1136
(Ceilings)

KENTILE FLOORS, INC.
58 Second Avenue
Brooklyn, New York 11215
Tel.: 212-768-9500
(Flooring)

BORIS KROLL FABRICS, INC.
979 Third Avenue, 2nd Floor
New York, New York 10022
Tel.: 212-755-6200
(Fabrics)

LARSEN, JACK LENOR, INC.
41 East 11th Street
New York, New York 10003
Tel.: 212-674-3993
(Fabrics and carpeting)

LEES CARPETS
Valley Forge Corporate Center
King of Prussia, Pennsylvania 19406
Tel.: 215-666-7770
(Carpeting)

LEVOLOR LORENTZEN, INC.
1280 Wall Street West
Lyndhurst, New Jersey 07071
Tel.: 201-460-8400; (Illinois)
800-322-4400; 800-447-4700
(Window coverings)

LOUVERDRAPE, INC.
1100 Colorado Avenue
Santa Monica, California 90401
Tel.: 213-450-6100; 800-421-6666
(Window coverings)

MECHO SHADE CORPORATION
42-03 35th Street
Long Island City, New York 11101
Tel.: 212-729-2020
(Window coverings)

MOHAWK CARPET
57 Lyon Street
Amsterdam, New York 12010
Tel.: 518-841-2211
(Carpeting)

OWINGS-CORNING FIBERGLASS
CORPORATION
Fiberglass Tower
Toledo, Ohio 43659
Tel.: 419-248-8182
(Acoustical partitions)

PYROLITE SYSTEMS, INC.
500 Jericho Turnpike
Mineola, New York
(Door hardware)

REPUBLIC STEEL INDUSTRIES
PRODUCTS DIVISION
1038 Belden Avenue, N.E.
Canton, Ohio 44705
Tel.: 216-438-5200; 800-321-0216
(Shelving)

H.H. ROBERTSON COMPANY
400 Holiday Drive
Pittsburgh, Pennsylvania 15220
Tel.: 412-928-7500
(Underfloor ducting)

SCHLAGE LOCK COMPANY
(PART OF WORLDWIDE
INGERSOLL-RAND)
2401 Bayshore Boulevard
San Francisco, California 94134
Tel.: 415-467-1100
(Hardware)

ISABEL SCOTT FABRICS
CORPORATION
245 Newtown Road
Plainview, New York 11803
Tel.: 516-249-3100
(Fabrics)

STANLEY HARDWARE DIVISION
195 Lake Street
New Britain, Connecticut 06050
Tel.: 203-225-5111
(Hardware)

SUPREME EQUIPMENT AND
SYSTEMS CORPORATION
170 53rd Street
Brooklyn, New York 11232
Tel.: 212-492-7777
(Files)

THOMAS AND BETTS
920 Route 202
Raritan, New Jersey 08869
Tel.: 201-685-1600
(Wiring)

UNITED STATES GYPSUM
COMPANY
101 South Wacker Drive
Chicago, Illinois 60606
Tel.: 312-321-3865
(Walls and ceilings)

Magazines: United States and United Kingdom

Administrative Management
51 Madison Avenue
New York, New York 10010

The Architect's Journal
9 Queen Anne's Gate
London SW1H 9BY

The November 11 and November 18, 1981, issues were a comprehensive review of office design.

Architectural Record
1221 Avenue of the Americas
New York, New York 10020

The Architectural Review
The Architectural Press, Ltd.
9 Queen Anne's Gate
London SW1H 9BY
Tel.: 01-22-4333

Building Operating Management
Box 694
407 East Michigan Street
Milwaukee, Wisconsin 53201

Building Owner and Manager
1221 Massachusetts Avenue, N.W.
Washington, D.C. 20005

Business Systems & Equipment
Maclean Hunter, Ltd.
76 Oxford Street
London W1
Tel.: 637-7511-8

Communications
1900 West Yale
Englewood, Colorado 80110

Contract
1515 Broadway
New York, New York 10036

Corporate Design
850 Third Avenue
New York, New York 10022
Tel.: 212-593-2100

Facilities Design and Management
1515 Broadway
New York, New York 10036
Tel.: 212-869-1300

Industrial Design
1 Astor Plaza
New York, New York 10036

Information on design for the handicapped, office products, and ergonomics.

Information & Records Management
250 Fulton Avenue
Hempstead, New York 11550

Interior Design
850 Third Avenue
New York, New York 10022

Also publishes an annual directory of sources of furniture and furnishings.

Interiors
1515 Broadway
New York, New York 10036
Tel.: 212-764-7300

Journal of Systems Management
24587 Bagley Road
Cleveland, Ohio 44138

Management World
Maryland Road
Willow Grove, Pennsylvania 19090

Modern Office Technology
614 Superior Avenue West
Cleveland, Ohio 44113

The Office
1200 Summer Street
Stamford, Connecticut 06904

Office Equipment Index
Maclaren Group
Davis House
69-77 High Street
Croydon CR9 1QH
Tel.: 688-7788

Office Equipment News
Business Publications, Ltd.
109-119 Waterloo Road
London SE1 8UL
Tel.: 928-3388

Office Product News
645 Stewart Avenue
Garden City, New York 11530

Office Systems
IPC Electrical-Electronics Press, Ltd.
Quadrant House
The Quadrant
Surrey SM2 5AS
Tel.: 661-3500

Progressive Architecture
600 Summer Street
Stamford, Connecticut 06904

Reproductions Review & Methods
401 North Broad Street
Philadelphia, Pennsylvania 19108

Security Management
2000 K Street, N.W.
Washington, D.C. 20006

Telecommunications
610 Washington Street
Dedham, Massachusetts 02026

Word Processing World
51 Madison Avenue
New York, New York 10010

Several magazines have had special issues devoted to office design: *Domus* (December 1979); *Technique et Architecture* (May 1981); *Bauwelt* (January 1977); *Interiors* (June 1981, the automated office); and *The Architect's Journal* (November 11 and 18, 1981).

Bibliography

The following is a selected listing of books and articles that deal with open or "landscape" office planning, plus a few general works on office design. Magazine articles presenting theoretical material on open planning are listed, but pictorial reviews of typical projects are not, except where they touch on general issues.

Bach, Fred W. "A Systems Approach to Ergonomics." *Modern Office Procedures*, October 1974.

Brief, Michael E. "Interior Plantscaping: What the Designer Needs to Know." *Designer West*, Vol. 28, No. 10, August 1981.

Caplan, Ralph. *The Design of Herman Miller.* New York: Whitney Library of Design, 1976.

The Carpet and Rug Institute. *Carpet Specifier's Handbook.* Dalton, Georgia, 1980.

Center for Fire Research, Institute for Applied Technology, National Bureau of Standards. Washington, D.C. 20234.

Cihlar, C., ed. *New Concepts in Office Design.* Elmhurst, Illinois: Business Press, 1966.

Cohen, Elaine and Aaron. *Planning the Electronic Office.* New York: McGraw Hill, 1983.

Consumers Guide, editors of. *Decorating Your Office for Success.* New York, Harper and Row, 1979.

Cowan, Peter, et al. of the Joint Unit for Planning Research, University College of London and the London School of Economics. *The Office: A Facet of Urban Growth.* New York: American Elsevier Publishing Co., Inc., 1969.

Delgado, Alan. *The Enormous File.* London: John Murray, 1980.

Duffy, Francis. "Interior Design: Future of Office Planning." *The Architectural Review*, June 1979.

_____. "Paper Factory or Room with a View?" *Architectural Review*, June 1979.

Fetridge, C., and R. Minor. *Office Administration Handbook.* Chicago: Dartnell Corp., 1975.

Fracchia, Charles A. *So This is Where You Work?* New York: A Studio Book, The Viking Press, 1979.

Friedman-Weiss, Jeffrey. *Working Places.* New York: St. Martin's Press, 1980.

Galloway, Lee. *Organizing the Stenographic Department.* New York: Ronald Press, 1924.

Gorb, Peter, ed. *Living by Design.* London: Lund Humphries, 1979.

Hall, Edward T. *The Hidden Dimension.* Garden City, New York: Anchor Books, Doubleday and Co. Inc., 1966.

Hamme, R., and D. Huggins. "Acoustics in the Open Plan." *Office Design,* September 1968.

Harris, David A. et al. *Planning and Designing the Office Environment.* New York: Van Nostrand Reinhold, 1981.

Heyel, C., ed. *Handbook of Modern Office Management.* New York: McGraw Hill, 1972.

Hewes, Jeremy Joan. *Workstead: Living and Working in the Same Place.* New York: Dolphin Books, Doubleday and Co., Inc., 1981.

Hjelm, Ake. "Subjective Spaces of Landscaping." *Office Design,* March 1968.

Joedicke, Jurgen. *Office Buildings.* New York: Praeger, 1962.

Joiner, Duncan. "Social Ritual and Architectural Space." In *Environmental Psychology, 2d ed.—People and Their Physical Settings.* Harold M. Proshansky, William H. Ittelson, and Leanne Rivlin, eds. New York: Holt, Rinehart and Winston, 1970.

Klein, Judy Graf. *The Office Book.* New York: Facts on File, 1982.

Kramer, Sieverts and Partners. *Open Plan Offices.* London: McGraw-Hill Book Co. (UK) Ltd., 1977.

Leffingwell, William Henry. *Office Management: Principles and Practices.* Chicago: A.W. Shaw Co., 1925.

Management Conference. *Improving Office Environment.* Elmhurst, Illinois: Business Press, 1969.

Manning, Peter, ed. for the Pilkington Research Unit. *Office Design: A Study of Environment.* University of Liverpool, Department of Building Science, reprinted 1966.

Mills, C. Wright. *White Collar.* New York: Oxford University Press, 1951, reprinted 1976.

Mills, Edward David. *The Changing Workplace: Modern Technology and the Working Environment.* London: George Godwin, Ltd., 1972.

Mogulescu, Maurice. *Profit Through Design.* Amacom, 1970.

Moskowitz, Milton, Michael Katz, and Robert Levering. *Everybody's Business.* San Francisco: Harper and Row, 1980.

Osborn, Alex F., and Robert E. Ramsay. *The Optimism Book for Offices.* Jamestown, New York: Art Metal Construction, Inc., 1918.

Palmer, Alvin E., and M. Susan Lewis. *Planning the Office Landscape.* New York: McGraw Hill Book Co., 1977.

Parsons, H. McIlvaine. "Work Environments." In *Human Behavior and Environmental Advances in Theory and Research,* Vol. 1, Irwin Altman and Joachim F. Wohlwill, eds. New York: Plenum Press, 1976.

Pentagram. *Living By Design.* London: Lund Humphries; New York: Whitney Library of Design, 1979.

Pile, John. "Clearing the Mystery of the 'Office Landscape'." *Interiors,* January 1968.

_____. *Interiors 3rd Book of Offices.* New York: Whitney Library of Design, 1976.

_____. "The Nature of Office Landscaping." *A.I.A. Journal,* July 1969.

_____. "The Office Landscape: Does it Work?" *Progressive Architecture,* June 1977.

_____. *Open Office Planning.* New York: Whitney Library of Design, 1978.

Planas, R.E. "Integrated Planning Concept." *Building Operating Management,* June 1973.

_____. "Yes: We Introduced it in this Country." *The Office,* July 1969.

Polites, Nicholas, ed. *Improving Office Environment.* Elmhurst, Illinois: Business Press, 1969.

Price, Judith. *Executive Style.* New York: The Linden Press, Simon and Schuster, 1980.

Propst, Robert. *The Office—A Facility Based on Change.* Zeeland, Michigan: Herman Miller, Inc., 1968.

Propst R., and M. Wodka. *Action Office Acoustics Handbook.* Zeeland, Michigan: Herman Miller, 1975.

Propst, R., M. Wodka, and J. Kelley. *Action Office Energy Distribution Handbook.* Zeeland, Michigan: Herman Miller, 1976.

Salmon, Geoffrey. *The Working Office.* London: Design Council, 1979.

Saphier, Michael. *Office Planning and Design.* New York: McGraw-Hill Book Co., 1969.

_____. *Planning the New Office.* New York: McGraw-Hill Book Co., 1978.

Schultze, Earl, and Walter Simmons. *Offices in the Sky.* Indianapolis: Bobbs Merrill, 1959.

Shoshkes, Lila. *Space Planning.* New York: Architectural Record Books, 1976.

Sommer, Robert. *Tight Spaces.* New York: Prentice-Hall, 1974.

"The Steelcase National Study of Office Environments: Do They Work?" Conducted by Louis Harris & Associates, Inc., 1978.

Steele, Fred I. *Physical Settings and Organization Development.* Reading, Massachusetts: Addison-Wesley Publishing Co., 1973.

Index